BUILDING A BUSINESS

CREATING A LIFE

A DESIGN FOR FINDING PERSONAL FULFILLMENT AND PROFESSIONAL SUCCESS

PENNY CARTER

SPIRIT PRESS

Portland, Oregon

SPIRIT PRESS
3324 N.E. Peerless Place
Portland, Oregon 97232

For Mom
your Spirit lies within us all

and for my dear friend, self-appointed
surrogate Mom and cheerleader,
Katie

Contents

Acknowledgments

I would like to offer special thanks to cheerleaders and dear friends: Katie Hartnett, Diane Duke, Sue Adams, Holly Oberg, Gail Karvonen, Sheri Boone, Marye Thomas, Marilyn Schulte, Anna Wiancko-Chasman, and Bill Scheider. Thanks to my Great Aunt and Uncle, Rose and Bud Casey for their belief in me enough to front a small business loan. Thanks also to my brothers, Todd and Steve; and their wives, Tammy and Leslie; and my lovely and talented niece, Emily who takes after her Aunt Pen; my nephews, Andrew, Scotlynd, Jon and Evan, the nephew previously known as Boo Boo. And special thanks to my Father, Joe, who quite often served as "Bank of Dad" while I was trying to start a business about which I was truly passionate. Thanks goes out as well to Edmondo Severa and all the baristas at Cafè Torrefazione Italia on N.E. 15th Avenue in Portland for keeping me in great coffee, embracing support and a never ending supply of welcoming smiles. Special thanks to, Bill Scheider for cover design, Chris Butzer for early illustrations (that did not get used!), to Bob Smith of Book Printers Network, and to Suzanne Deakins of Spirit Press for her guidance and expertise in the overall process.

I would also like to offer special thanks to Fern Gorin, M.A. and the Life Purpose Institute for her insight and formal training in the Life Purpose

Process©, to Dr. Lynda Falkenstein for her encouragement and support, and to Michael Donnen, wherever you may be.

Introduction

Building a Business—Creating a Life offers a framework on which to build a business from the inside-out. It asks you first, to build a foundation of self-knowledge and helps put that knowledge to work for you in a very practical way.

You might have picked up this book because you want to create your business, well, a little differently. You want to find personal fulfillment and you want to be professionally successful in every aspect of the word. Up until now, you may have thought those two were mutually exclusive. That's simply not true! You can have them both. The difference is, you get to do it your way. Doing it your way means doing business in congruence with who you are…with integrity. The catch is, in order to do business in congruence with who you are, you first have to know who that is. Only then will you be able use that information in a practical way in building your business.

You may already know what kind of business it is you would like to start or expand upon. The exercises and questions in this book will either validate that for you or will challenge you to ask, "Is this really what I want to be doing?" It will also give you insight as to, perhaps, a more personally fulfilling and viable option.

My intent for this book is to help you make the connection between who you are, what you have to offer and how you do it to create more meaning, purpose and success in your work. It takes trust on your part that the pieces of the puzzle will ultimately fit together. It involves taking risks. Risks of self-discovery that hold information to enrich and enliven your life.

I hold a core belief that each of us has uniquely expressed gifts and talents. When those gifts and talents are combined with the many facets of our own, unique identities (our discovered and defined values, our personality traits, our passionate ideas and causes) we begin to unlock the keys to our life's true work.

Part One:

Under Construction

Chapter 1

Breaking Ground

———— ▪ ———— ▪ ———— ▪ ———— ▪ ———— ▪ ————

To know others is understanding.
To know self is wisdom.

Lao Tzu
from the Tao Te Ching

How Self-Knowledge Holds the Key to Personal Fulfillment and Professional Success

Socrates said "an unexamined life is not worth living." Think about what that means for a moment. I'm not talking "touchy-feely" connotations. I'm speaking about the deep introspection and contemplation of who we truly are, why we're here, what we want our lives to stand for and how we're going to make that happen. Granted, it's not typical American dinner-time conversation. But it's conversation we need to be having with ourselves.

If we don't know who we are, if we don't know what it is we want our lives to stand for, how can we possibly find meaning, purpose and fulfillment in our personal or work lives?

Many of us are finding less joy and passion in our work and, subsequently, in our souls. Many of us have become disenchanted. The passion and ideals we originally brought to our jobs are no longer there. We have an innate desire, and, truly a need, for more meaning and sense of purpose. We've awoken to find that somehow, somewhere along the line, we have been seduced into accepting society's definition of success instead of defining and living it for ourselves. In other words, we'd been living our lives for someone else. We're just coming around to the realization that we've been prostituting ourselves at the expense our own spiritual, psychological and personal lives. No wonder we don't want to get out of bed on Monday morning!

The signs of disenchantment are clear. You might find yourself getting ill on a frequent basis— whether that be head or stomach aches or something more serious. You may have lost interest and enthusiasm for things you once held passion. You might be wishing you were someone or somewhere else and having constant thoughts about your place in the world. You might have difficulty sleeping, have recurring dreams or simply just don't want to get up. And, in order to put all of this out of your mind, you might be indulging a bit more than usual in alcohol, food or drugs.

There is, however, a paradigm shift taking place in America. There seems to be a collective inner yearning that is challenging each of us to re-define ourselves according to who we really are and to discover and realize our unique true life's work.

Some of us will decide that it's worth it to take some risks and begin to build a business that allows us to give our gifts and talents in a way that is congruous with who we are. Most of us don't have the first idea of what it is we want to do or how to go about finding out. This book will help you.

So how do you go about defining yourself and building a business that is a natural expression of who you are? You start by gathering pieces of the puzzle or the unique elements of your true self. Only then, after you have a solid foundation of self-knowledge can you put that information into practical application and assemble the pieces into an integrated "whole" puzzle.

This book offers insight on three key areas you'll need to examine when building a business from the inside-out.

First, you need to make a conscious effort to define yourself. Be honest with yourself about working through the questions and be open to the process, (i.e. expect some surprises about yourself!). Ask yourself the question, who am I? And hang in there long enough to unearth the answers. It's not fair to say what you do for a living or what your roles in life are, for example a mother, student, or caregiver. That's not to say the role is unimportant. It's just not what you're asking. Ask yourself, what am I about? What are my core values? What values did I inherit from my family or religious institution? Take a hard, meaningful look at them. Try them on—like a hat—for size. Are they truly your values? Or, have you simply accepted them because they were presented.

Ask yourself what moves or motivates me? What things, causes, ideas or people am I passionate about? These can be vital in discovering your life's true work.

Take a look at the things you do naturally. What are your natural talents? I don't mean "learned" skills, but what do you do well with a complete sense of effortlessness? One question I ask groups is "what did you used to get in trouble for on a consistent basis when you were growing up?" (Voicing your opinion? Talking? Taking things apart?). Chances are, if you got in trouble for it on a consistent basis, it's something that came quite naturally to you. This question, too, can hold a tremendous amount of insight to your true and "natural" life's work.

Second, you'll need to be able to pragmatically apply the information you've learned about yourself as well as practical information about the business you intend to build. You'll be taking a look at your business from all the angles—your client or customer's, you competitor's, your supplier's, as well as the businesses that enhance your business. You'll also need to utilize that information to help you find your own unique sense of identity in a tight, cluttered and often chaotic marketplace. In addition, you'll need to explore how you will market yourself through traditional and, if appropriate, Internet marketing opportunities, creative alliances, and by building authentic professional relationships.

Finally, you'll need to look at some "finishing touches." When we begin to make changes in our lives, many of us encounter fears...fears of failure, success, inadequacy, change, risk. These fears produce "blocks" that paralyze us and cause us to throw up barriers to our own success. You'll need to learn to first identify and then address these fears and learn how to take calculated risks that will spawn growth and success.

Anytime change is a factor, we run into what I call the "demolition crew"...a group of quite possibly well-meaning people who, because of their own fears and blocks, may unconsciously attempt to undermine your success. You will also need to know how to identify members of your personal crew, set boundaries around them and how to stay in a state of "self-referral" instead of allowing their words to influence you.

Congratulations! You've come this far. Now, let's start to lay the foundation of self-knowledge.

Who are You? Laying a Foundation of self-knowledge

Okay. You can be honest. After hearing the suggestion that the key to personal fulfillment and professional success was self-knowledge, you silently chuckled and whispered "yeah, right." Right? I know that not too many years ago I would have.

. . . Yet something, some desire or yearning motivated you to pick up this book. Perhaps you heard a radio interview about the book, or read a review. Maybe a single phrase struck a chord within you that inspired you to take a closer look. Or maybe that entrepreneurial spirit with which you were born simply said "it's time." Whatever the reason, pat yourself on the back and know that you have taken the first step to—as Tom Cruise said in the film Jerry Maguire—being the "me I had always wanted to be."

Why self-knowledge?

First of all, anytime you have a service or product to sell, you aren't actually selling the service or product. Okay, you are. But every one of your clients or customers can buy that service or product from someone else besides you.

What is it that will motivate the client to invest hard earned dollars with you? I'll tell you. It's the assurance that the client can trust you to do what you say you are going to do, on time and at the price you've quoted.

How does the client make that decision? By experiencing your self-confidence, passion for your work, integrity, and by having established an authentic professional relationship with you.

What does that have to do with self-knowledge? Knowing who you are, what you want your life to represent, and how you intend to achieve the goals to get there inspires self-confidence, creates greater passion and purpose for what you do, produces a strong sense of self and inspires you to live with integrity…to live in congruence with who you are. So what you see is what you get. The client can trust this. The client can trust YOU!

self-knowledge has even greater practical application. It can help you decide what it is you truly want to do—if you haven't already decided it. It can also help you find your niche—your unique sense of identity in the marketplace once you have decided what kind of business you will create and will help you determine how you do your business.

These next few pages are filled with questions and exercises that will encourage you to take a profound look at yourself and how you see your place in the world. The information will be enlightening and empowering. As you go through these exercises, don't try to figure out how the information is going to be used. You'll drive yourself crazy! Right now, what you're trying to accomplish is to create pieces of the puzzle. We'll worry about assembling it later on.

It's a Value You Hold. But Is It Yours?

Do you know what your values are? And, once stated, can you honestly say they are truly yours?

Most of us tend to hold onto values that have been instilled since childhood by social institutions like our families, schools, peers, religious organizations, and, as we become more ingrained into society, even corporations.

Many of us accepted these values simply because they were handed to us. We never questioned the values or ourselves to see if they truly "fit" who we were.

The process of discovering and defining your values may be challenging at first, but the rewards are immeasurable.

Identifying and naming your true values will help you understand why you may be uncomfortable in certain situations, or why you prefer to work in one environment over another. Values hold the key to our inner-most absolute truths about who we are.

Before we set out to discover and define your values, let's first get a working definition of what a value is. A value is a principle by which you live your life. It is a strongly held concept or belief. It is a way of knowing and believing that subsequently influences your actions.

Your values are unique. You may share some common universal and cultural values, but you possess unique values that help shape and define who you are.

The following exercises will help you gain a greater awareness of yourself. Some of the answers may even surprise you. I'm certain that after you sit with them for awhile, you'll come to respect yourself for who you truly are even more.

Your Values Defined: The Exercises

The following questions are meant to be answered at a time when you can sit quietly, without interruptions and think deeply about the answers. You may want to work on one question at a time over a period of days or even weeks.

To get to the "core" of your answer, keep asking yourself "why is it that I feel this way?" This will help you more specifically define your most closely held values.

After a few of these questions, you will begin to see themes. These themes are a representation of your core values.

1.   How do you define happiness? What brings you joy? Is it having time for contemplation? Is it the sound of a baseball bat cracking as it connects with a fast ball? Is happiness spending time with your family or

completing a project successfully at work? However you define it for yourself is right and it holds keys to your values. Ask yourself what about that is important to me?

_____

_____

_____

_____

2. How do you define success? How you define success says a great deal about who you are and what you value in life. You may define success as having enough wealth to do the things you've always wanted to do, send your kids to college, travel, have a home on the northern California coastline. If this is the case, you may be surprised to understand that your values are not necessarily about money, but rather they may lie in providing for your family, education, and serenity. Ask the question, what's behind how I define success to find the value.

_____

_____

_____

_____

3.   What does it mean to be "authentic?" What does it mean to you to be "real?" What does that "look like" for me when I am being authentic? Again, these answers hold keys to your values. Keep asking what's behind it.

_____

_____

_____

_____

4.   If you were the wise man or wise woman and people came to you for advise, what three gifts of wisdom would you give to them? This is similar to the previous question, but worded in a way that may elicit a different set of answers.

_____

_____

_____

_____

5.   What are the behaviors that other people do that absolutely drive you crazy? (We always have fun with this one.) When I ask this question in workshops, I tend to get a combination of knowing laughter and puzzled looks. The laughter because WE CAN ALL

THINK OF BEHAVIORS THAT OTHER PEOPLE DO THAT DRIVE US CRAZY! And puzzled because they can't quite figure out how it relates to values. It relates very well, thank you. When you identify a behavior that drives you crazy, take a look at the opposite behavior. That will identify a value for you.

For example, you can't STAND IT when others cut you off in mid-sentence and interject their thought instead. It drives you NUTS! You feel dismissed. You feel unacknowledged. You feel unimportant and that what you have to say has no value. UGH! Take a look at the opposite behavior. You are allowed to express your thoughts fully and explain the reasoning behind your statement and people even ask you follow-up questions! Wow! So what is that? For me, it would mean that what I had to say was important, that my opinion and experience were valued and that the other individual had RESPECT for me and my beliefs. Now, here's where identifying the value can be a bit tricky. That same scenario may hold different values for other individuals. That's great. They're supposed to. That is your uniqueness shining through. The word respect may have entirely different connotations for someone else. Language is relative. That is why it's so important that you identify your own values and not rely on someone else to do it for you!

_____
_____
_____
_____

6.   What is something about what you do that you hold to be an absolute truth? For instance, as I mentioned before, I hold a firm belief that the key to personal fulfillment and professional success is self-knowledge. What about what you do that you hold to be an absolute truth?

_____
_____
_____
_____

Now, once you've answered these questions, go back and highlight the themes you see in them. These will be your core values. Most of the other values will be able to fit under one of these core headings. Many of these answers will also hold keys to your passions.

The questions in this next exercise relate to working for others as well as working for yourself. All of the answers hold valuable information, can validate your current business direction, and offer you some clues as to why you may have become disenchanted with where you've worked in the past.

Please rate each value as:

3—Vital   2—Very important
1—Situationally important   0—Not important

__ *Autonomy:* Work independently and without a great deal of direction from others.

__ *Intellectual Challenges:* Be actively involved with complex questions and problem-solving.

__ *Creativity:* Be involved in the design and development of new ideas, programs, campaigns or complementary marketing materials, speeches, or training manuals.

__ *Creative Challenges:* Look for new and resourceful ways in which to accomplish a job.

__ *Competency:* Express a high degree of competency and knowledge: consistently demonstrate effectiveness.

__ *Work with Public:* Have daily interaction with people.

__ *Decision Maker:* Have authority to make key business decisions and develop and implement policy.

__ *Sense of Security:* Prefer knowing you have a steady, stable income rather than working at a commission-based position or for yourself.

__ *High Energy:* Work under fast paced, time-pressured circumstances.

__ *Excitement:* Work under conditions that are exciting or that involve a high degree of innovation or field-specific breakthroughs (science, academic, economics)

__ *Team Work:* Work with a group of individuals with a clear direction and set, common goals.

__ *Inspire Others:* Have the opportunity to inspire others to be their best and to lead them in your directed course of action.

__ *Help Others:* Providing direct service, either individually or in small groups that offer financial, emotional or spiritual aid to others.

__ ***Supervise Others:*** Provide direct supervision to and have the responsibility of work done by others.

__ ***Status:*** Being held in high regard in your chosen field by peers as well as being seen as successful in the eyes of others.

__ ***Affiliation:*** Be recognized and respected as a member of or affiliated with a particular organization.

__ ***Validation:*** Receive acknowledgement, both publicly and privately for work well done.

__ ***Financial Validation:*** Receive financial validation for the work I perform at a level that will allow me to live comfortably and experience the areas of life that are my passions.

__ ***Flex Time:*** Have control over my own schedule and the ability to change it as necessary.

__ ***Authenticity:*** Work in congruence with my values, natural talents and passions even during difficult times.

__ ***Integrity:*** Walk my talk in personal and business dealings and form authentic, professional relationships with clients or customers.

__ *Passion:* Work in a setting that will reflect my passionate interests.

__ *Use of Talents and Gifts:* Utilize my natural talents and gifts in my work.

__ *Make a Difference:* Use my work to contribute to social betterment.

__ *Get Physical:* Use bodily strength or dexterity in work.

__ Precision: Perform tasks that require precision work and accurate attention to detail.

__ *Variety:* Having work responsibilities changed frequently in content and setting.

__ *Stability:* Have a work routine and job duties that are largely predictable and not likely to change over long periods of time.

__ *Completion:* Be involved in projects that have a start and a finish versus ongoing program management.

__ *Taking Risks:* Feel comfortable and excited about taking calculated risks to achieve financial and personal growth.

__ *Competition:* Be able to challenge myself against my competitors or work associates in a healthy manner to inspire growth and opportunity.

__ *Sense of Community:* Be actively involved in community projects through volunteer work or politics.

__ *Physical Location:* Live in an area conducive to my work and lifestyle.

__ *Artistic Expression:* Be able to express myself through my chosen art forms and, if desired, have it provide an income base for me and my family.

Go back and make a list of all of your "vital" values.

Please list your top 7 here:

1. _____   2. _____

3. _____   4. _____

5. _____   6. _____

7. _____

Hopefully, you are seeing some general "themes" from these questions and the last exercise.

Keep a list of these value themes. We will refer back to them later.

I know when I first answered these questions, I felt validated. I may not have been able to "name" all of my values before hand, but answering the questions in the way they were posed and doing the exercises helped me to understand why I've felt uncomfortable in certain situations and thrived and grew in others.

These exercises do say a great deal about who you are. These are your values. When you honor and live by your values, you honor and respect yourself. By demonstrating respect for yourself, others will know this and respect you as well.

How Your Passions Play a Role in Your Success

Without passion in our lives, our souls begin to dry up. We simply go through the motions.

When I speak to others about what I do and about what I believe to be true for me, one of the most important impressions I want to leave with them is that of a woman with passion. Passion for the work I do. Passion for love. Passion for life!

Most of the time that passion exudes sponta-neously and effortlessly. Even on days where self-doubt has a hold on me, when I speak from the heart and from a place of passion and self-truth, my energy level immediately rises and I am soon filled with that energy that illuminates the outward expression of passion.

Haven't you listened to someone who is so excited about what he or she does that it's infectious? That is what I mean by passion.

After one of the free lectures I gave on building a business and creating a life, most members of the audience agreed to exchange business cards. One man, in his thirties, who had stated during the talk that he has many business cards and uses them all—depending upon the given situation—didn't have any of these cards on hand to exchange. I don't think that he wasn't interested in networking and simply decided not to pass them out. Rather, I believed—from the things he had said and the way in which he had said them—that while he could do many things, he had no passion for any of them. Or, he might simply have been so over extended that he had no energy left for the areas of work he truly enjoyed. My question for thought to him was, "are you doing what you really want to do?"

There happened to be another man in the group who offered similar services and who was very excited about it! Guess who would have gotten my business that day? Yep. The one who was apparent in his passion for work and who had clarity on just what it was that he did.

Passion also comes into play in another important way when you're first starting a business. There will be some lean times. The person with passion for the work and a vision for success will have the "stick-to-itiveness" that is needed to get beyond those times.

Passion Factor Exercises

Again, please take some quality time when asking yourself these questions. Enlisting the help of a supportive friend or family member can also help if you get stuck. Ask these questions of them about you.

1. What causes or issues are you most passionate about?
    I have been involved with children's grief issues for many years. It is something for which I hold a great deal of passion. I am also dedicated to helping others define who they truly are and to live from that authentic base. Friends of mine are impassioned environmentalists. The environment is at the heart of who they are. Getting and receiving exceptional customer service may hold a tremendous amount of energy for you. I have a completely unscientific theory that says if we all paid attention to who we were —our passionate interests, values and natural talents—and acted upon those things, all of the issues in the world would be taken

care of. Instead, we tend to do what's expected of us—whether that be by our parents, spouses, society. I'm for doing life differently!

---

2.   What are some things that cause you pain or that create a visceral reaction within you? In other words, what are some things that really push your buttons? For most, any kind of abuse is simply something that is intolerable—whether it involves humans, animals, the environment. Everyone is different about what they are passionate about. There are no right, wrong, or better answers.

---

3.   What are the things you love to do? What brings you joy? What are the things that shout "I am alive!" when you do them? What is it you do that makes you feel alive?

_____

_____

_____

_____

4.   What do you want your life to stand for? A simply worded question. But one that is loaded with passion and values-based answers. For example, I want my life to stand for passion, wisdom (worldly knowledge as well as inner wisdom), integrity, authenticity, inspiration and humor. All of those things are values I hold and things about which I am truly passionate.

This question is also a wonderful "centering" question. When I have needed to make a decision, either in my personal life or career, I have asked myself—"will what I am proposing to do support what I want my life to stand for?" When you ask yourself this question, the answer is usually quite apparent.

_____

_____

_____

_____

You've got a Talent for That! And Why it's Important

I've said it before. Yet it bears repeating. We each have natural talents and gifts and we each have a unique way of expressing them. When we pay attention and honor these gifts through our work and/or play, we find that life isn't about struggling. It's about living it! It's a lot easier to go with what we have instead of going against it. It brings a deeper meaning to the phrase "go with the flow."

I've had people argue with me that they simply didn't have talent for anything! I think many of us get caught up in what "talent" is. We may tend to think of talent being something only artists possess, or athletes. Not so, dear friend. Artistic expression and creativity come in many forms. You might not have the ability to draw, but you have a way with organizing a room so it's aesthetically pleasing and functional. Cooking and presentation is an art form. If we get stuck in thinking we all have to be Van Goughs to be considered creative or expressive, we're not paying attention.

You may have a talent for public speaking, organization, problem solving, mediation, book-keeping, etc. You most likely can also identify what you don't have a talent for, or passion, for that matter. I have no idea how a computer operates. . . how much memory it has (or even what that looks like—megs or rams or whatever)...AND, I don't care, frankly. I only care that when I turn it on, it works. I am fortunate to have a patient brother (Todd) and former colleague (Russ) who answer what I can only assume are the most simplistic questions one can ask about these things.

Another thought I'd like to express about talents is that while you may possess a talent, you may not want to use it in your career. That's great! You don't have to! It's there for your enjoyment when you want to use it. You also don't have to try to utilize all of your talents at once. Some talents will be expressed while others will lie dormant for a few years while, for instance, you raise children.

Natural Talents and Unique Expression Exercises

Again, you may want to enlist the help of others. Sometimes we are so close to our own situation that it's difficult to identify something that comes so naturally as a talent.

1.   What comes naturally to you? What is it that people are always coming to you and asking you to do for them? I've had clients say that people come to them to listen to their problems. They don't see how that's a

talent. Active, empathetic listening is a talent that takes a great deal of present moment awareness. Some people get asked to organize garage sales. That could demonstrate a talent for organizational skills, presentation—how the merchandise is displayed—and communication in talking with the bargain hunters. So, ask yourself the question and then think of all the skills necessary to do this task. Then ask yourself if the skill is something that comes naturally or did you struggle to have to learn to do it?

2. What did you used to get in trouble for on a consistent basis while you were growing up? I also like this question. For some people, it can be a difficult question to answer. For others, it may bring a chuckle. My brother, Todd—computer guru and electrician—used to get in trouble for tearing things apart to see how they worked, because, at least when he was young, he couldn't always get it back

together. He's a gifted electrician with an intense passion for computers. It's made a powerful combination in his successful career. There was a young woman in one of my workshops who said she always got in trouble for not doing her homework. How could that possibly point to a natural talent, she asked? I asked her what she was doing instead. She was writing stories. She'd get in trouble for having her head up in the clouds, too. This woman was a gifted writer! We do have our own answers. We simply need to know which questions to ask and where to look.

3. What are the things you got praised for when growing up? This can be a tricky question, because a lot of what we got praised for we did because we needed to get along in the world. Ask yourself if it came naturally, or if it was something you felt you had to do. You

can also try to ask yourself what are the
things you felt you should have gotten
praised for.

_____

_____

_____

_____

_____

_____

4.   Take a look at your resume. What skills are
     listed? Ask yourself what, if any, of these
     skills come naturally to you. Sometimes
     we overlook the obvious. Looking at how
     you've presented yourself to potential
     employers in the past can have hidden
     clues.

_____

_____

_____

_____

_____

     Go back over your lists for values, passions
and natural talents. Make a one page synopsis of
your findings so that you can have easy access to
them later on.

Values:

_____

_____

_____

_____

_____

_____

Passions:

_____

_____

_____

_____

_____

_____

Natural Abilities:

_____

_____

_____

_____

_____

_____

_____

Experience, Education and Passion In Your Field of Business

You may hold the passion for something. Let's say, opening a neighborhood coffee shop. That passion may even support a value of yours. It's quite possible that you might also have a natural talent for selecting gourmet coffee blends and making people feel welcome and at ease. Everyone you know says you should open your own coffee shop. You believe you can be build a successful business because of this. And, maybe you can.

However, you need to know that simply having a passion and talent for something does not necessarily mean you'll automatically be successful building a business around it.

There are some other things you'll need to take into consideration. You'll need to answer questions such as what do you really know about your chosen field? Is there room in the market for you? Who do you know in that field who might be able to help you get started?, and, what kind of life and work experiences have you had that relate to building a business in general such as marketing skills, management, or accounting.

You may have the passion. You also need the practical.

Education, Field Experience and Training

Let's say you've decided to start a business renting VCRs and videos to senior citizens. You have a stock of new and used VCRs, and literally hundreds of films, both classic and contemporary from which your client can choose.

You don't have experience in VCR repair, but have been a movie buff for years and have worked for five years as a video store manager. You've received a small business loan from an elderly supportive uncle who feels there is a need for such a service. You've purchased the videos and VCRs, have a van and a list of retirement centers. You're set, right? Well, not quite.

You've got to address the following issues:

How will seniors know of your service to begin with? Do you know how you are going to market your business? Do you know where to begin? Do you have a marketing plan? Do you know how to develop one?

Let's say the marketing issue is addressed. You've only made plans to drop off the VCR and video. What about those folks (of all ages!) that don't know how to hook up the VCR? Will you take the extra time necessary to set it up and show them how to run it? Is that figured into the cost of the rental? Oh! You haven't determined the cost of the rental yet. You need to figure in your time, vehicle expense, storage rental, cost of the VCR and video, liability, health and car insurance, etc.

What if a VCR breaks down? Do you know how to repair it? Will you hire someone else from the outside to repair them? Will they make house calls?

Your find your senior clients have special needs relating to your service. Are you equipped to handle them? Do you know who to call? Are you aware of other services available for seniors if you should see a need?

I've created this rather simplistic scenario to stress a point. You many have a keen interest and even passion for what you have decided to do, but if you do not have the experience, training or education, (if necessary) you may run into trouble. That doesn't mean you shouldn't or can't do what you want to do. It does mean that if you are going to take the risk of building your business, you'll want to make that risk a bit more calculated by getting experience and training in the field.

Doing so will also help you determine if it is truly what you want to do and you'll be better equipped to transition into your own business with a foundation of experience, training, self-knowledge and education.

A friend of mine, Bill, at the age of 51, decided he was burned out in his current career in counseling. He had a passion for environmental issues and decided he was going to become a "green" gardener. He had no experience or knowledge in the field, had never owned his own business or hired employees, couldn't differentiate weeds from exotic plants and hadn't the first clue as to what kinds of "green" mixtures he would need to take care of clients' gardens. It sounds like a recipe for disaster. But Bill was determined and decided he would learn as he went along. He signed up for classes at a local community college in business, horticulture, and environmental studies. He practiced on his own lawn and garden and worked for another firm for a designated time—until he could become licensed. Today, he is turning away business. He operates under a value of fewer clients, better quality. He also requires that his clients sign an agreement stating that while their garden is under his care, they will not use chemicals. He will not subject himself, his employees or his dog to exposure. He and his clients operate under an umbrella of mutual respect.

Passion, desire, commitment and gained experience all contributed to his success.

Go back and look at your resume. Think about the work you did and think of what it really translates to. Did you do the books for a small firm as part of your job? Did you help with an ad campaign? Did you design a special promotion around a product or service? Were you able to gain insight and information as to the how and why of these tasks? Are you open to learning more about each of these areas? Write your thoughts here:

Life Experiences

Life experiences, any life experience, can be adventurous, exciting, inspirational, or heart-felt. They can also be traumatizing, gut-wrenching, burdensome or devastating.

And, while we're in the middle of them, the last thing we are thinking of is "how's this going to benefit me when I start my business?"

Let's look at some life experiences that you are now on the other side of.

Make a list of as many life-changing life experiences that you can. Your wedding day, your divorce, winning a marathon, your long-awaited trip to Europe, the death of a loved one, the birth of a child.

This exercise is as pertinent for those of you who aren't certain as to what kind of business you would like to start as it is for those of you who are certain.

To the right of each event on your list, make notations as to how the event changed you. For example:

Winning a marathon	Now want to inspire others to go for it! I did it, so can they!
Death of a parent	Embarked on a deep spiritual quest.
Trip to Europe	Realized I could reach a goal, despite financial obstacles.

Now, to the right of the notation, make a list of lessons learned, skills obtained, wisdom gained that could be used in developing ideas for a new business and/or enhancing the operations of an existing business. For example:

Marathon	inspiring others	Personal and Professional Coach
		Inspire employees to set/achieve personal and professional goals
Parent Death	spiritual quest	Counsel others who endure the death of a parent.
		Being able to have an experiential understanding of what an employee might be going through and help in reassessment of job duties and expectations for the near future.

| Europe | reach goal despite financial restrictions | Consult with others on money management and/or ways to save and how to be resourceful |
| | | Finding creative ways in which to pay the business' expenses while continuing to build it. |

The point here is to get you to look at your life experiences in new ways. To, perhaps, re-frame the event as a life's lesson learning event and to take that information and build upon it in both your personal and work life.

Who You Know

I hate to say it, but who you know does count. The more people you know in your given field, the better off you'll be. The good news is, if you don't know anyone, you can always go out and get to know them.

Join and attend professional associations with monthly meetings and "mixers." Find out the key players in the field and request informational interviews. Ask those people you do know who they know in the field and if they'd be willing to introduce you. Get to know who you need to know.

The more people you know—you talk to—you ask advice from—the more people who are able to join in your success!

Part Two:

The Form, Function and Structure
Of Your Business

Chapter 2

Framing Your Business

The dream or vision is the force that invents the future.

James M. Kouszes and Barry Z. Pozner
from *The Leadership Challenge*

First, Envision Success, Your Way

Now, I'd like to ask you to return to the values section and re-visit the question: How do you define success? As I mentioned, how you define success for yourself says a great deal about who you are and what you value in life. It can also tell us how you might choose to "do" your business.

I'd like you to expand upon that answer. I'd like you to envision success. Your success. What does that really look like? Write it down in a workbook for yourself.. Consider all of the other values that you've identified to help you see yourself in your successful career and life. Consider "success" in all aspects of the word. Include your

personal or family life, how you would conduct
business on a day to day basis so that you are in
congruence with who you are, how much money
you would make, and what you will do with it. If
you plan on hiring employees, how would you relate
to them? How would you lead and inspire them?
Which natural talents would you like to express and
how do you want to express them?

Remember, personal fulfillment and professional success are not mutually exclusive! You get
to "do" success however you define it.

I am a firm believer that in order to achieve
success, you must first envision it. Now that you
have a clear vision of yourself, let's take a pragmatic
look at how you're going to get there.

Walk a Mile in Their Shoes: Stepping into the Roles of your Clients, Competitors, Suppliers and Enhancers

I lived in the Washington, D.C. area for over
four years and worked at an events management
firm. It was early on in my career when I was asked
to sit in on an important client meeting. The client
was a large firm and wanted to bring its top sales
persons to the Nation's Capital as a reward. They
had a pretty clear idea of what they wanted in the
way of special evening events and tours. The client
was trying to convey this to one of the principals of
the firm, when the principal literally interrupted the

client and said "You don't want that! Let me tell you what you want."

I wanted to shrink and slide out under the conference room door! One very important lesson I had learned from earlier sales, marketing and public relations positions was LISTEN TO WHAT THE CLIENT HAS TO SAY AND TO WHAT HE OR SHE WANTS! NEVER TELL THEM WHAT THEY WANT!

You can certainly make suggestions, if requested, and, in specific instances, you can correct a misconception they may have, but I'd really stop short of being the expert for their company.

What you can do, however, is to find out as much as you can about the client or customer, what challenges or issues they face, and answer the question "where are they coming from?" or, "what's their operational framework?" You'll then be better equipped to make suggestions that will fit their needs and make you look informed and in a position to help them.

You can also identify and step into the shoes of all the players in your business game to gain a better understanding of the overall picture. There are more players than just you and your client.

There are those companies who provide you with the "raw" material for your product or service—in other words, your suppliers. There are your competitors. You need to know what they're up to and what they're not up to in order to find opportunities that will build your business. And, there are those companies or individuals whose product or service enhances your product or service. I call them "enhancers."

First, we'll start with your clients or customers. (I'll use the terms clients and customers interchangeably. A client is someone who buys a service from you. A customer purchases a product.)

Who are Your Clients and Where are they Coming From?

Do you know who your client is? If not, that's the first thing you need to know before you can get your product or service to them.

To get started, you'll want your customer to meet at least some general criteria:

- They will already know about what you are selling (product or service), won't need to be educated about it, and will want to have it.

- They have the income necessary to purchase your product or service.

- They are willing to buy the product or service from you.

Also, ask yourself:

What kind of individual or business will want my product or service?

_____

_____

_____

How will my product or service benefit them?

_____

_____

_____

What are the characteristics common in individuals or businesses that need my product or service?

_____

_____

_____

_____

After you've answered these questions, test your answers. Go out and interview potential customers or clients. Ask them if they currently use a similar product or service. This is also a great time to find out what's missing for them in the product, service or customer service. Where there's a hole, there's an opportunity!

You'll want to go to a place where you are likely to find your potential customer or client. If your customer is another business, call the company and find out who handles purchases of your product or service and request an informational interview. Again, it's a wonderful opportunity to learn what needs are not being met.

If you are marketing to individuals, try to get as much information as you can. This will help you when you design and implement your marketing plan. Get to know your clients.

Ask them:

What newspapers, trade or consumer magazines, newsletters, journals, etc. do they subscribe to and read? You may want to look into paid advertising, news releases for free talks, or information on article submissions to these periodicals.

What professional groups do they belong to? There may be an opportunity at a local level to present at one of their meetings, or to purchase a mailing list. You can also find out about regional and national meetings, presentations and/or booth space, if appropriate for your business.

What community groups do they belong to? Which charities are they involved with? You may want to consider a promotional event that benefits a charitable organization of which both you and the client/customer are fond.

Which businesses do they currently get a similar product or service from? Are they happy with the product or service? Are they happy with the customer service surrounding the product or service? What's missing? What do they feel can be added to the product or service to enhance its value? Remember, where there's a hole, there's an opportunity.

How did they find out about the product or service? To what mode of communication do they best respond? (calls, direct mail, free talks, in-person visits, email?)

_____

_____

_____

_____

Are they aware of your particular product or service? How did they hear about it?

_____

_____

_____

_____

What are your professional/personal (depending upon product or service) challenges or issues? Are they being met? How can you see these as being met? These questions can give you clear insight as to the problems and potential solutions faced by your clients.

_____

_____

_____

_____

If you're meeting with a business, frame questions so that they reflect the business arena:

What trade magazines, newsletters, or journals are relative to your industry? This question is important because those periodicals will address current challenges and issues faced by companies in this area of business. You'll want to know this information in order to determine if what you offer will help meet those challenges, or if you can tailor what you offer to do so.

_____

_____

_____

_____

What trade or professional conventions do they attend? You can find out from the association if there are opportunities to display information or make presentations.

_____

_____

_____

_____

From whom do they currently get a similar product or service? Are they happy with the product or service? Are they happy with the customer service surrounding the product or service? What's missing? What do they feel can be added to the product or service to enhance its value? Again, where there's a hole. . .

How did they find out about that product or service? What mode of communication do they prefer? You'll want to respect it.

Are they aware of your particular product or service? How did they hear about it?

What are current trade trends, challenges or issues? Are they being addressed?

If you're having trouble with any of this, remember. YOU are also a client or customer of someone else. What are the things you look for in a service or product and in the customer service surrounding the product?

Now that you're armed with information about your client, let's move on to your competitor.

Who Are Your Competitors and What Are They Doing?

You are truly unique and your business is a unique reflection of who you are. So, you really don't have any competition, right? Well, no, not exactly. You are unique and so is how you do your business AND so too, are your competitors unique in their style and presentation. Your competitors have found their unique sense of identity in the marketplace. Knowing what that is will help you establish yours.

I will first ask you to identify your competitors. Use the information gained from interviewing your clients or customers. Use the yellow pages if necessary, or a trade directory. Ask around. Then, shop around. Do business with your competitor? Yep.

Ask a friend if you can use his or her name and address and call each competitor to send information on the product or service. Drop by the competitor's retail outlet or visit current retail establishments that offer the competitor's product for sale. Ask questions about the product and the supplier (your competitor). Find out what retailers are saying about the competition.

Key questions you are going to want to find answers to are:

Who are my competitors?

_____

_____

_____

_____

What are my competitors doing?

_____

_____

_____

How are they doing it?

Are they meeting our mutual client/customer's needs?

How do they handle customer service? Are they meeting or exceeding customer service expectations?

Who, exactly, are they serving? What is their niche?

Who, exactly, are they not serving? Where's the hole? This could be your niche.

Do your competitors have services or products that you do not have, but can possibly contract with them to complete your client's project? (It's been known to happen, folks).

The key here is to find out as much information as you can. I love the bumper sticker that says knowledge is power. Knowledge is power in business, too.

Who Are Your Suppliers and How Can You Help Each Other?

Who are your suppliers? What is a supplier? A supplier is an individual or business that supplies you with the tools you need to do your business. Tools might include fabric if you have a clothing line, caterers if you are an events planner, medical supplies if you are a doctor, software if you are a graphic designer or a phone company if you are a sales person.

What's interesting about suppliers is that while you are in essence a client or customer of the supplier, there can also be hidden opportunities for cooperative marketing. So let's get a list started. You can always add to it as they come to mind.

Ask yourself what tools you use in conducting your business. Make a list of the tools on the left side of the paper. To the right of the tool, list the supplier. For instance, an upscale laundromat/coffee shop certainly uses washers and dryers, laundry detergent dispensing machines and individual size boxes of laundry detergent as well as dryer sheets and fabric softener. It also uses an espresso machine, coffee maker, filters, cups and saucers, coffee, sweetner, milk, flavors, etc. Each one of those "tools" has a supplier.

Tools   Supplier

_____   _____

_____   _____

_____   _____

_____   _____

_____   _____

_____   _____

Now, make a second list. List the supplier and then any potential creative cooperative opportunities you can think of. For example:

Supplier	Cooperative Idea
CleanClothes laundry detergent	Free Soap Friday—to bring in customers for you and get them to try/buy suppliers' soap. (supplier brings the soap!)
Torrefazione Italia Coffee Blends	Guest Baristas from local shops and free coffee drinks from 2–5 PM—typically your laundromat's slowest time.

Now, your list:

Supplier	Cooperative Idea
_____	_____
_____	_____
_____	_____
_____	_____
_____	_____

_____   _____

_____   _____

_____   _____

_____   _____

_____   _____

Don't think that your idea is too crazy or too complicated. You never know what cooperative dollars are available out there to do special promotions. Look into it!

Remember to give yourself the gift of utilizing your natural talents. These promotional events are wonderful opportunities to do so and can make them more fulfilling for you!

Who Are Your Enhancers?
And Why You Should Care.

What are enhancers and, why should you care? Enhancers are other products or services that add value to your product or service.

Returning to the example of our upscale laundromat/espresso cafe—carts on wheels bring extra value to the laundromat. They aren't necessary, but they add an element of convenience. It also doesn't hold much appeal if customers have to sit in lawn chairs and drink from plastic cups. Wonderfully designed ceramic mugs and comfortable chairs create a special atmosphere. The live musicians you may hire on Friday evenings enhance the ambiance and contribute to the overall experience of what is a typically boring routine.

An enhancer is something that when used with your product or service brings added value to your product or service.

Enhancers, too, can offer an opportunity for creative alliances. Complete the same exercise as you did above for the suppliers. Create your list of enhancers and the contact person for that enhancer. (Some enhancers may also be suppliers!).

Enhancer   Contact Name

_____   _____

_____   _____

_____   _____

_____   _____

_____   _____

_____   _____

_____   _____

_____   _____

Now, repeat the second step. List the enhancer to the left and any creative ideas of cooperation to the right.

Enhancer/Contact   Cooperative Idea

....

....

....

....

....

....

....

....

....

....

....

Can you see how simply taking a look around you can help you with some great marketing ideas? I'll go over some basic marketing strategies and tips in chapter four.

Who Are You and What Do You Want Your Life to Stand For?

I want to return to this at the end of each chapter because I believe it is the essential question you need to keep asking yourself. At every step, at every junction in your business building process, I'd suggest you re-visit the question and stay directed and focused on your goals. It will help you build the business you truly desire.

_____

_____

_____

_____

_____

_____

_____

_____

_____

Chapter 3

Framestorming

━━━ ▪ ━━━ ▪ ━━━ ▪ ━━━ ▪ ━━━ ▪ ━━━

Out of chaos comes brilliance.
Chinese symbols for chaos and
brilliance are the same

Establishing Your Unique Sense of Identity in a Tight, Cluttered and Chaotic Marketplace.

When I speak of your unique sense of identity in a tight, cluttered and often chaotic marketplace, I speak of your niche.

A niche, in architectural terms, is described as a " recess in the wall." So, you might ask, what does a hole in the wall have to do with where you fit in a marketplace? It has everything to do with it! Because, where there's a hole, there's an opportunity!

A niche is a special area of demand for a certain product or service. For your product or service!

This chapter walks you through the steps of "Framestorming." That is, taking the information we've outlined in the previous chapter and really working it—live and in person with some of your suppliers, enhancers, supporters, and even your competitors.

Getting the Information You Need

There are several ways in which you can go about gathering the information that will help you in establishing your unique sense of identity— your niche.

You can, as I've outlined below, hold a focus group to gather this information, or you can request an informational interview from each participant at their place of business, using the outline in this chapter. There are pros and cons of each.

Visiting the participant at his or her place of business saves time and trouble for the participant. However, in a small group setting, you are more apt to generate stronger ideas simply because of the fact that you have a live, interrelated of group people discussing your business! Group interaction is dynamic and, I believe, much more can arise from this framestorming process!

Let's set the stage:

Identify a group of individuals from your list of clients or potential clients, suppliers, enhancers and competitors outside of your market area, if possible.

Name	Company
_____	_____
_____	_____
_____	_____
_____	_____
_____	_____
_____	_____
_____	_____
_____	_____
_____	_____
_____	_____
_____	_____

Generate a letter asking for their expertise in identifying current trade trends and challenges and in generating ideas as to how these might be addressed within your market area. Let them know you are starting a business and would like to be well-informed as to how your business will best meet the needs of clients and work best and identify potential opportunities of mutual benefit with enhancers, suppliers and competitors.

Your ultimate goal is to have a group of 6-8 people representing each related area to your business. You may want to call before the letter goes out to assess interest and then use the letter as a confirmation. Or, you may prefer to send the letter as a way to open the door and then make the follow-up call. Always be respectful and appreciative of their time.

Don't worry if you aren't able to get a representative from an "out of the area" competitor to attend. You can get this information by "shopping" the competition, as mentioned in chapter three.

Be sure to choose a time and location that is convenient to most participants. It's great if you can meet in a quiet room of a restaurant and host a meal. If not, comfortable office surroundings and snacks and beverages are acceptable. I prefer to meet in person for a forum such as this, however, conference calling is also an option. You might consider having a gourmet box lunch delivered along with an agenda or outline of the call prior to the time of the call.

The meeting itself should have a clear focus. It should also start and end at the pre-arranged times. Remember, these people are professionals who have agreed to give you their focused attention. Be respectful of their time.

The outline of the meeting might look like this: (you may wish to alter some questions so that they more specifically address your field).

You may also want to do one of two things, record the meeting—with the permission of the participants, or ask a supportive friend or colleague to take copious notes. You want to listen to what is being said, but not be distracted by trying to get it all down. Write the highlights for yourself and jot down any follow-up questions that come to mind when someone is speaking.

Welcome and thank participants again for their time, expertise and creative input. Restate the purpose of the meeting. Address any "house-keeping" details (such as restrooms, food and beverage, phones, etc.).

Ask each participant to introduce themselves and say how they are affiliated with your business.

Offer a brief overview of the "framestorming" session and then get started quickly.

Below is a list of key questions you will want to address. You want to be able to gain information that will help you in identifying clients or customers, help you decide on how you will market yourself and give you insight as to where or what specific group or niche you will market to. Give each participant who has something to say, time to say it. However, you must be able to facilitate the meeting efficiently. By that I mean, if the talk is getting too far off track, you need to be able to diplomatically pull it back in and on track. The questions may be few, but the time it takes to answer them thoroughly may surprise you.

What are current trade trends?

_____

_____

_____

_____

_____

What are current challenges or issues being faced?

_____

_____

_____

_____

_____

Are they being addressed? How are they being addressed nationally/locally?

_____

_____

_____

_____

_____

Clients: Are you happy with the product or service? Are you happy with the customer service surrounding the product or service? What's missing in either the product, service or customer service? What do you feel can be added to the product or service to enhance its value? How did they find out about that product or service?

_____

_____

_____

_____

How are competitors in your market area meeting the needs of clients?

_____

_____

_____

_____

How are suppliers and enhancers working with competitors in marketing efforts?

_____

_____

_____

_____

What makes the competitors unique? What is their niche? What isn't?

_____

_____

_____

_____

_____

If you feel you are not getting enough information from your questions, or that the participants aren't as vocal as you had hoped, re-phrase the questions and ask "what about that is of particular concern?" or "what do you think is the reason for that?" You are bound to unearth some interesting answers.

Following the group—remember to end on time—thank your guests again and if you have not opted to host a dinner, you might consider presenting a small, useful gift that is appropriate to the business—between $10-25 each. You want to make it nice enough so they know you are truly appreciative of their time, but not too elaborate as to lead them to believe something is expected in return.

I am also a firm believer in hand-written thank you notes. I know there are those who will disagree in this age of email, but nothing stands out more strongly to me than someone who has taken the time to hand-write a note.

Framestorming   − 71 −

Synthesizing the Information

Now that you've gained the details you'll need, let's take a look at and synthesize the information. Go back over the notes to your meeting. Use the following outline to organize your answers in your notebook:

1. Current Trade Trends

   ....
   ....
   ....
   ....

2. Current Trade Challenges/Issues

   ....
   ....
   ....
   ....

3. National Approaches to Challenges/Issues:

   ....
   ....
   ....
   ....

4.   Local Approaches to Challenges/Issues:

_____

_____

_____

_____

_____

5.   *Clients:* What's missing in the product or service they receive?

_____

_____

_____

_____

6.   *Clients:* What can be added to the product or service to enhance it and better meet your needs?

_____

_____

_____

_____

7. *Clients:* How do they find out about the product or service?

_____

_____

_____

_____

_____

8. Are/How are competitors meeting the needs of clients?

_____

_____

_____

_____

_____

9. Are/How are suppliers and enhancers working with competitors in marketing efforts?

_____

_____

_____

_____

_____

10.   What's unique about what the competitor has to offer or the customer service?

_____

_____

_____

_____

_____

11.   What are local market competitors' niches?

_____

_____

_____

_____

_____

Now, go back over these answers. Take a look at what clients/customers want and need. Are those needs being met? Can they be met in a different or unique way? What are the things you can add to your product or service that will enhance its perceived value?

Where's the hole? There's the opportunity!

Holes   Opportunities:

_____   _____
_____   _____
_____   _____
_____   _____
_____   _____
_____   _____
_____   _____
_____   _____
_____   _____

Who Are You as a business? Setting Boundaries to Achieve Your Goals

It's not quite as simple as discovering where the holes are and plugging yourself in there. Well, it is and it isn't. Aye, there's the rub.

Many of us, when we're first starting out in a business and are faced with more monthly expenses than income, will start to expand our reach as to what we do and what we don't do in our businesses. We've got to pay the bills, right? That's true AND what's also true is that the more you expand—when you're not ready to - the more diffused your efforts and the less likely you are to succeed.

That doesn't mean you can't change the focus of what you're doing—especially if you've found the niche isn't really a niche at all. You need to change it. But, to return back to the example in chapter two with the man with multiple business cards, if you don't have a clear picture of what you do or offer, neither will your clients or customers.

At this point, I'd like you to answer the following questions and to return to them as often as necessary to find that focus.

How do you define your business? What kind of service or product do you offer?

_____
_____
_____
_____
_____
_____
_____
_____
_____
_____

How don't you define your business? What kind of services of products do you not offer?

_____

_____

_____

_____

_____

_____

_____

_____

_____

_____

What kinds of business are you willing to give up in order to remain focused and to achieve your unique definition of success?

_____

_____

_____

_____

_____

_____

_____

_____

_____

_____

How will you address clients/customers stated needs if it's not something you want to focus on or have the current ability to do so?

At what point will you change the focus of your niche when you discover a new one?

Who are You and What do You Want Your Life to Stand For?

I want to keep bringing you back to reevaluate these questions. I challenge you to begin thinking about the questions as they relate to what you are doing in your business and how you are operating your business.

Ask yourself these questions: Who am I? What do I want my life to stand for? Ask the follow-up question: How will what I am doing in business or how I am conducting business help in accomplishing that?

Write in your notebook specific examples of ways in which you will conduct business to live and work authentically and with integrity:

_____

_____

_____

_____

_____

_____

_____

_____

_____

Chapter 4

Your Business Facade: How Will You Market Your Business?

*The philosophy behind much adver-
tising is based on the old observation that
every man is really two men—the man he is
and the man he wants to be.*

William Feather
(American author and publisher)
From *Quotable Business* by Louis E. Boone

*The most powerful element in adver-
tising is the truth.*

William Bernbach
(Founder, Doyle Dane Bernbach Advertising)
From *Quotable Business* by Louis E. Boone)

How Do You Want to be Recognized?

A great deal needs to be taken into consideration when deciding just how you will market
yourself and your business such as your target
market, the needs of the clients or customers in that

market, how you will differentiate yourself from your competition, and, how you want to be seen.

My belief and bias, of course, is that your business façade and personal identity need to match. In order to find personal fulfillment and professional success, your business needs to be a reflection of who you are. Having and operating your business in congruence with your values and convictions brings personal satisfaction and fulfillment. It also promotes and breeds integrity—which is what your clients and customers are looking for.

To get an idea of what I mean by how you want to be recognized, take a few moments and complete the exercise below.

To the left are the names of individuals and corporations. To the right, write in the first word that comes to mind when you think of this person or company.

Bill Clinton

Bill Gates

Tom Brokaw

Steven Spielberg

Egghead

Kinko's

Barnes and Noble   _____

Walmart   _____

Pottery Barn   _____

Starbucks   _____

Amazon.com   _____

I think that even with these few names you are beginning to get an idea as to what I'm trying to convey. How do you want to be thought of? How are you going to make that happen?

Two Words on Business and Marketing Plans: Have them!

You have an incredible idea, the knowledge, experience and passion to see it through. You have an idea as to what it will cost you to get it up and going and at what point you'll really start making a profit. You've done the numbers and run the spread sheets, so you're pretty sure everything is set and you don't really need to go through with that silly little exercise in futility called a business plan, right? Wrong.

Going through that silly little exercise in futility can help you determine if you have a viable business. It can help to point out holes in your plan.

It forces you to set goals and state how you will achieve those goals. It forces you to look realistically at projected sales, income, profits, expenses and monthly cash flow.

The benefit of going through the exercise of a business plan is that you begin to get a more realistic idea of and feel for your business.

It's true that viability in a business can only be affirmed in a real-world test, but the more "bugs" you can work out ahead of time, the more likely it is that your business will survive and prosper.

Contained within a business plan is a marketing plan. Thinking through a marketing plan thoroughly and seeing it on paper gives it power. It also creates energy and enthusiasm as you begin to see the possibilities!

While creating a business and marketing plan are beyond the scope of this book, I will say they are necessary elements to the success of your business. The exercises you completed in the previous chapter will help you identify cooperative marketing ideas and opportunities which you can add to your overall plan.

Excellent software programs exist on the market that walk you through each step of the process. If you're new to marketing plans, I'd really recommend purchasing one of these.

Defining your Market

You'll want to revisit the definition of your client or customer and where the holes are in the marketplace in providing your product or service. You'll want to choose a niche that is unoccupied. It's a lot easier to fill a hole in the market place— you can market without competition—than to seduce customers from where they are being well served. . . if they are being well served.

Outlining your Reach

Where will you market your service or product? Will you limit yourself to the local area or will you try to gain a regional, national or global reach? That's okay if you want to. Make a conscious choice to do it, if that is your desire. But just know that the Internet, telephone services and mail order catalogs make regional, national and global opportunities within reach of just about anyone.

If you offer consulting services, you might consider faxing or overnight expressing necessary written materials and talk via the telephone. You can market yourself via the Internet, other major cities yellow pages, and/or newspapers, if appropriate.

If you sell a product, you might consider offering the product over a secured web site. While the "hot" items to purchase via the Internet continue to be computers, computer software, books, entertainment and music, that does not mean you cannot offer your product.

If you are serious about this, I would hook up with a firm that designs and markets web pages. They are the experts in making it easy for others to find you. You'll want to market your web page via traditional marketing vehicles as well like your brochures and business cards, telephone messages, yellow page ads, and any other form of advertising or promotion you do.

Discovering other Potential Sources of Income

A mindset that many just starting out tend to hang onto is that there is only one source of income with our service or product. Get out of that already!

There are many potential sources of income that can derive from your initial product or service. It simply takes a little thought and creativity.

For example, that upscale laundromat could host live music on Friday nights and charge a cover charge—with a portion of the proceeds going to the owner's favorite charity. It could also gain additional sales from biscotti, scones and other wonderful treats that compliment coffee and espresso. Since it's upscale, why not offer concierge services - taking care of everything from getting a car serviced to restaurant and hotel reservations or whatever your client base has said they would be willing to pay for. You might also consider a pick up and delivery arrangement with a dry cleaning service.

The consultant certainly offers one on one consulting. There are also opportunities for workshops, paid speaking engagements, developing and certification of a particular "process" that is used, writing, marketing and selling a book and, perhaps, even a radio program or "minute."

The senior video rental service can have a store front and rent to the general public as well. It can offer snacks on delivery. It can market gift certificates to sons, daughters and grandchildren to give to older relatives and friends. (It might be able to work with a local senior services division as well as local churches on special projects that may generate these sales).

I don't want to get too far away from working in congruence with who you are. I'd suggest you ask yourself if these are the kinds of marketing ideas you'd like to implement and if you feel okay about them. I would go into a gratis project because I wanted to, not based solely on the assumption that I might get clients or customers from it.

You might also consider "cause" marketing. Cause marketing includes events or promotions that include a financial benefit for a particular "cause" or non-profit organization. I would suggest selecting a cause or issue which holds passion for you and something to which you would give time and/or money to without involving your business. People will know, respect and respond from that passion and sense of genuine concern.

Relationship Building: It Takes Time!

People buy people. They buy trust, follow-through and integrity. They can get the service or product from someone else, so who you are, how you do business and your uniqueness will count. Get to know your client/customer as you would a friend. Be genuine when you cultivate a professional friendship. You want to build a relationship built on mutual respect and knowledge.

From a marketing standpoint, knowledge is power. The more you learn and know about each client, the better you will be able to anticipate their needs and desires and you will be better able to market to them in a manner in which gets their attention and motivates them to buy from you! I can't stress enough, however, not to tell them what it is they need. You can make suggestions, but please don't assume that you know what is best for them.

Listen!

You can tell when someone on the other end of the phone line isn't quite giving you his or her full attention. It's frustrating, especially if you really want to be heard. And, in some instances, it can be hurtful.

The same holds true in a client relationship. Many clients or customers leave their current service or product supplier because they don't feel heard. Worse still, they may feel ignored and unimportant. A client or customer wants to feel as important in your eyes as that $100,000 client down the road. Listening is the first step in building successful professional relationships.

Listening, active listening is part art and all heart. When you are listening to a client or customer, listen to them with the openness and heart that you listen to a close friend. Reflect back to them what they are saying. This does two things. First, it lets them know you are listening. Second, it helps you to clarify something they are saying—especially if you are not quite following them.

Remember the simple courtesies such as not interrupting. Make mental, or even written notes of questions you want to ask. Don't interject with your story—unless it's pertinent to the conversation. It's not your agenda! Don't try to top their story.

These seem to be simple suggestions, but I will tell you many people don't use them and it will show in how many clients or customers they lose because of it.

Learn!

The Framestorming you completed in chapter 3 will help you gain insightful information necessary to begin building your business relationships. You want to learn as much about each customer as you can. This will help you better design and implement a marketing plan.

In addition to the Framestorming questions, you'll also want to discover specific information relative to the individual or business client:

- What are their distinct problems, challenges, issues?

- How do they prefer to be contacted and how often?

- What are their preferences in products or services?

- How do they find out about services or products when they need them? Use that medium!

Give Good Customer Service!

Excellent customer service is a vital element to building and maintaining professional relationships.

I've read recently, that on average, a corporation loses half its customers within five years. Knowing that it costs more money to acquire new clients or customers than to retain them, doesn't it make sense to have a good customer service program?

If you have ever purchased a book from Amazon.com, you have experienced excellent customer service.

You go "shopping" on the Internet, place your selections in a shopping basket, verify your order, see when and how it will ship, and proceed to the check out stand and pay with your credit card via a secured site.

Almost immediately, you receive an email confirming your order. You are also told if a book is not currently in stock, when it will be in stock and when it will ship. The day it ships, you get another email. If a partial order is shipping the email will indicate that and let you know when the remainder of the order will ship. The day the remainder of the order ships, you get another email, letting you know it shipped, how much it was and the shipping cost.

They also send you book marks (a very appropriate and great way to market/advertise) upon which a wonderful quote is printed .

In other words, folks, they stay with you until your order has been successfully completed! They stay in contact. You stay informed. That's what it's all about.

As a customer, I get most frustrated when I know I'm being given the run around and not facts.

I am a reasonable person and know that timelines get blown out of the water and "business life" happens just as personal life happens. If I am kept informed and given truthful information about what is happening with my order, I can make appropriate changes in my plans if necessary.

Here are some "basics" in giving great customer service:

- Keep in contact with your client/customer and let them know what's going on with their order.

- Be genuine in your concern that their needs are being met.

- Give unexpected added values.

- Offer free samples, seminars, speaking engagements.

- Make sure working in congruence with who you are and quality are at the forefront of what do you.

- Deliver when you say you will and do what you say you will—practice integrity!

- If you didn't quote it, don't bill for it. No one likes surprises. You can let the client know you left it out of the bid and you will still honor the bid. There are instances, of course, where that is simply not possible. In this case, I would provide truthful, accurate information and make every attempt to keep the customer satisfied—even if this means suggesting another service or product supplier if you cannot meet expectations.

- Sponsor preferred customer events and hold open houses with food and beverage to get together in a social setting with clients.

- Thank you notes (mail, email, call) within 48 hours of a purchase or service completion.

- Many people keep track of birthdays (month and day only) and send cards. (If you ask for their birthday—do something with it! I have had many businesses ask for the month and day of my birthday only to not use it. For some reason I remember that. Perhaps your clients/customers will too.).

- Be convenient. Set up a merchant VISA, MasterCard, and/or American Express account. Make it easy for your clients/customers to acquire your product or service. Secure an 800 number and make sure clients out of the local area know it! Offer an on-line catalog or order processing if it is appropriate to your business.

- Implement a referral award program. Request referrals and thank them when you get one (note and free offer).

- Send out quarterly newsletters with valuable information, upcoming events and product offers.

- Send out a Follow-up questionnaire—ask them for their opinion and   suggestions about your service, product. Use the information to improve your service.

- Maintain your client's confidence as you would a friend.

Creative Alliances to Increase Fulfillment and Income!

Creative alliances can enhance, build and give your business that additional edge over others in the field. Establishing creative alliances takes a little thought and has the potential to offer big rewards.

First of all, you want to identify other businesses (with products or services) that are looking for the same client or customer as you. You can start with your suppliers and enhancers. But don't limit yourself! If you've done the research on your client, you know what other types of products and services they purchase.

Let's go back to the upscale laundromat. The owner may have determined that his clients value time and would pay to have their car detailed instead of doing it themselves. The owner starts a "small details" Saturday promotion with a local detail shop. They come on site to detail the car for a special price. The laundromat may also get a percentage of the detail shop's sales for the day. If the detail shop advertises regularly, it may support the special day by mentioning it in the ads or sending a mailing to its regular clients. Virtually free marketing and increased income and traffic for the laundromat.

The senior video delivery service may decide it wants to offer a public service by sponsoring a day a month where free, on-site cholesterol screens are performed with every delivery. This can be done with a local hospital, non-profit organization, or senior services agency. These organizations would notify the seniors they serve through their own newsletters and advertising. Again, free promotion and a wonderful service. The video delivery service might decide to sponsor a meal a day on an ongoing basis with a local senior food delivery agency. In exchange, the owner would be able to distribute flyers and special promotional information on the route.

A consultant has a wide variety of opportunities—depending upon what type of consulting business is operated. The key is to know what other products and services your client/customer purchases and simply pick up the phone and make an appointment to speak with whomever's in charge of that product or service marketing.

Know What Your Business Is and What it Is Not

There will be times, especially when you are first getting started, that you will want to expand the scope of your product line or service to include that one additional thing your client needs. You'll be doubly tempted if your bills have yet to be paid and the client offers you half of the payment up front. While we will all do what needs to be done to keep the business going, I urge you to carefully consider the consequences of acting too quickly.

You may make a great deal of money in the short term, but you are also more likely to lose sight of what it was you wanted to do in your business in the first place. When that happens, you also lose sight of your uniqueness and then, yourself and what it was you wanted your life and business to stand for.

I'm not saying never take advantage of opportunities. I am saying to make a conscious decision about them and to make time to check in with yourself about your company's direction and purpose.

Remind yourself of the core of your business. What is it, specifically, that you offer? Who are your clients? Be cohesive in the marketing of your business to your customers or clients. If you're confused about who you are and what you offer as a business, your customer will be, too.

Who are You and What do You Want Your Life to Stand For?

Here we are again. As you begin to gather ideas for your marketing plan, I once again challenge you to consider how the question relates to what you are doing in your business and how you are operating your business.

Revisit the questions: Who am I? What do I want my life to stand for? How will what I am doing in business or how I am conducting business help in accomplishing that?

Write in your notebook specific examples of ways in which you will implement your marketing to live and work from an authentic base and with integrity.

_____

_____

_____

_____

_____

_____

Part Three

Finishing Touches

Chapter 5

Blocks: The Fears That Hold Us Back

There is nothing with which every man is so afraid as getting to know how enormously much he is capable of doing and becoming.

Soren Kierkegaard
Taken from *Zen and the Art of Making a Living* by Laurence G. Bolt

While I was researching quotes to use at the beginning of chapters, I came across several on taking risks. However, none were more profound than this by Kierkegaard.

How true it is that many of us are so afraid of knowing...of discovering and realizing our full potential.

We may have an inner yearning and conscious desire to soar—to live according to who we truly are, to reach out and grab life with all it has to offer—yet, we don't. We quite often resign ourselves to a life that has been carved out for us by others…and further underscored by life circumstances. We tend to believe that this is our "lot" in life and there is no way to transcend it. So when an opportunity does present itself, or when we create an opportunity, we tend to fall back on our limiting beliefs that say we can't do it— whatever it is.

Those old "tapes" begin to play in our head on automatic rewind. They ask us "who do you think you are, believing you can do this?" or suggest we really aren't competent or capable of moving beyond where we are.

We become fearful that what these tapes are saying is really true, and, in that fear we begin to build barriers to our own success. When we come to realize this, we can no longer place the blame outside of ourselves. Actually, we don't need help building barriers from anyone else. We do an outstanding job of it ourselves.

A "block" is something that prevents you from taking the necessary steps toward achieving your goals and realizing your full potential.

There are two major types of blocks that affect your success. They are what I call "your basic garden variety" or factual blocks and the more difficult to identify and work with "exotic" blocks. Exotic blocks are based upon deep rooted feelings or tightly held and integrated beliefs.

Both forms of blocks can be devastating both personally and professionally if you don't take time to identify, acknowledge and work on transcending them.

Garden Variety Blocks: Just the Facts

I call these "garden variety" blocks because, just like garden snakes, they are at first sight scary (at least for me, just ask my brothers who chased me around the yard with them), but relatively harmless. They may seem larger than life, dark, slimy and evil, but, when taken in at least one archetypal interpretation, they are really a symbol of wisdom. They have a message for us. The message is usually to take the steps necessary to change what you're dealing with. And, that, simply stated, is a fact.

That fact might look like: a) "I don't have the money to be starting my own business, b) "I don't have the experience necessary to expand my scope of services," c) "I don't have the professional accreditation to do that."

As overwhelming as some of those may seem, they are, relatively easy to work with. Facts are tangible. They can be easily identified, stated and transcended. Some may take a while to transcend, but the path to do it is usually pretty clear.

For example, most people don't have enough money of their own to invest into starting a business. Yet they still do it. This issue can be addressed by listing the options for obtaining other forms of financing. . . supportive family members, trusting friends, a bank loan or line of credit, or grant funding (if applicable). Ask friends, family and professional friends/associates for their ideas. Check out the Web. Call the Small Business Administration. There is money available to start businesses and you might be surprised where you will find it.

Not having the experience necessary to expand your scope of services is, too, a relatively simple issue to transcend. Go get the experience! Take necessary classes, work part-time for someone else in the area you wish to expand, volunteer to gain experience, work with select clients on a gratis basis while you are developing the service until you feel you are ready to begin charging a fee for it. Yes, it will take some time and it's doable!

Obtaining professional accreditation is on the same line of reasoning. Find out what you need to obtain it and then set a goal to achieve it.

Many people will need to juggle the needs of work and family life. It can be done. Keeping the lines of communication open while you are stretching to grow is important. It is also important for family members to know where they fit into the picture. How can they support you? Will there be time for them? How will this change benefit them in the long run? How will it help the family? Know and express the answers to these questions. Also, know and be aware of the times when you and your family need to come first.

Exotic Blocks: A Mystery Unveiled

The word "exotic" conjures up an air of mystery. These kinds of blocks are often a mystery to those who are experiencing them. They may know they have difficulty or feel uncomfortable with certain issues, but they are clueless as to what the cause behind it may be.

Exotic blocks, or blocks based on feelings or long-held, although often

misguided, beliefs, are more difficult to first identify and then to transcend. Most people don't fully transcend them. However, they do come to terms with them by acknowledging them, and making conscious choices about whether or not they will allow that particular block to prevent them from taking a next step that day or not.

I love the quote by M.A. Radmacher-Hershey that reads:

Courage doesn't always roar.
Sometimes, courage is the quiet voice at the
end of the day saying 'I will try again
tomorrow.'

Identifying and Working with Garden Variety Blocks

As I mentioned, identifying the factual or "garden variety" blocks are relatively easy when compared to the exotic blocks.

I would ask you to keep a journal of the statements you make to others and to yourself about why you cannot do something that will help you reach your desired goals. Do this for a period of one to two weeks. Enlist the help of friends, family members and those with whom you work that you trust to "call" you on certain statements you may make to them. Write these statements down as well. You may also discover some "exotic" blocks along the way. Keep track of these on a separate page.

The factual statements you may catch yourself saying to others and repeating in your mind may look like:

- I don't know anyone in that organization, how am I supposed to approach them?

- I don't have the money to join that professional association, even though I know becoming a member will be a catalyst for my professional growth.

- I can't apply for that job. I don't have the experience they require.

    Next, I would ask you to "challenge" each of those statements or thoughts you made to yourself or someone else. List the thought or statement on the left side of a sheet of paper. On the right side, write the "challenges" to it. For example:

- Don't know anyone

    I don't know anyone. But I can ask other business professionals or friend and family members in the trade if they do. I can also find out what trade associations are common in the field and start attending meetings to gain information and contacts. And, I could cold call to the HR department to find out names of individuals to speak with. I can then say that "Jon in HR suggested I speak with you."

- Don't have enough $ to join

    I don't have enough money to join the professional group. However, joining will allow me to take the classes I need at a reduced rate. It will give me the opportunity I need to meet others in the field and stay apprised of current issues in the industry. I can re-visit my budget to see where I can cut back or let go of other items that are no longer serving my needs. I could also see about "scholarship memberships" for new businesses. I could also ask a friend or family member to loan the money to me. Since I need to secure a small business loan anyway, I could add it to the budget I present to the bank.

- I don't have the experience
  I don't have the necessary experience listed on the contract. However, I do have experience where the skills will transfer well. It may not be what they are looking for in this contract, however, I will be able to demonstrate the abilities and experience I do have. Also, if afforded an interview, I will be making another contact in the field. I can also ask about other organizations who need the same type of work and who are willing to hire someone with a lesser degree of experience to gain the experience. I could volunteer at a non-profit organization and learn.

The object is to see how the statements that you make to yourself and others, although factual, do have solutions. We are often so close to our own situations that we cannot see them.

Your Blocks: Your Challenges
                                 to Them:

_____   _____
_____   _____
_____   _____

_____   _____
_____   _____
_____   _____
_____   _____
_____   _____
_____   _____

If you need more room, please use another sheet of paper. We're often quite amazed at the number of blocks that we have!

Another thing that can happen is that once we begin to identify and overcome "factual" blocks, we might find that those factual blocks have really been covering up deeper "exotic" blocks. Our reasons for not taking action may look factual, but the root may actually be located within an "exotic" block. And we thought we had ourselves figured out!

Affirmations

I am also a firm believer in daily affirmations. When we integrate positive thoughts into our daily patterns, those thoughts—over time—become our "default" thoughts. . . not the negative lines we're used to tossing out.

There are many books available with affirmations relating to specific issues. These are wonderful, AND I would ask you to write some of your own. I have mine written and laminated and I carry the card in my wallet. Whenever I need a reminder of who I really am and what it is I want to accomplish, I pull out the card and read through the statements. It really does work!

Identifying and Working with Exotic Blocks

As I mentioned before, exotic blocks are more difficult to identify and more challenging to work with. These blocks usually stem from issues that were born in our childhood and continued to get reinforced along the line—usually because of our own insecurities around them.

One of the more common exotic blocks is the "unwritten contract." Both men and women can have these contracts. Until they make a conscious decision to tear them up - mentally or literally - they will continue to haunt them and prevent them from achieving their full potential in both the personal and professional arenas.

Having said that, the simple act of tearing them up doesn't mean they go away. But having the awareness that they are there takes most of the power out of them.

An unwritten contract may be an understanding that was established early on in your life. A lot of times, these contracts are made with family members. Some examples of unwritten contracts might be:

- I will not be better than, more educated than, more successful than _____(fill in the blank). (it could be your father, mother, brother, sister, cousin, etc.)

- I will be an _____ (attorney, doctor, accountant) just as every other member of my family before has been.

- I cannot pursue my dreams of becoming a _____(veterinarian, police officer, business owner) because those aren't suitable jobs for women in my family.

Let's look at some possible reasons behind why the contracts may have been made in the first place. Perhaps then we can discover if hanging onto them is truly in your best interest.

Contract # 1:
- I will not be better than, more educated than, more successful than _____(fill in the blank). (it could be your father, mother, brother, sister, cousin, etc.).

There are several different ways in which to look at this contract. It might have been established because your father, mother, brother or sister is the "shining star" in the family and to surpass them would mean that his or her star is a little less bright.

This contract had been reinforced through school as you worked hard to be a member of the Honor Society, a star on the track team or even earned a full scholarship to the college of your choice—only to be told "it was more difficult to be admitted in the Honor Society when _____ was in school, _____'s track record was stronger or , "that school is okay, but it's not _____ the school _____ went to."

You learned that even though you tried hard to impress your family—those efforts were made in vain. Eventually, you accepted your role within the family and your self-confidence began to wane. You began to tell yourself you didn't have the ability to do something and, you began to believe it.

You may have continued to allow it to be reinforced because, well, we all need and want to be accepted in our family. When we know and accept our places within our family structure, life is much easier and we feel loved. You would have lost the love and support of your family if you had actually lived out your dreams and potential.

Now, when you ask yourself if the reasons you continued to allow the contract to be reinforced are still valid, you might have to answer no. Your _____ is retired, has gone on to other things, has discovered he or she was living his or her life for others and has changed paths. Even if the answer is yes, ask yourself if your unhappiness is worth continuing to adhere to the contract?

Many people will be able to talk to the individual with whom the contract is made. Those who do may find that that individual did not make the contract in a conscious effort to undermine you. Many times, people take part in these contracts in order to protect their own image and insecurities. It most likely had nothing to do with you—except that you may have been a threat to them.

The other side of this contract my be that someone is born into a family that has not seen a member go to college, make an income beyond lower middle class, or break away from working for the "company store" and live and work authentically.

This, too, can be extremely threatening to some family members. They may try to reinforce the contract by making statements that set you apart from the family or make you feel like a traitor. Remember, it's not you! It's most likely their insecurities that are prompting this behavior. Knowing this can help you set some boundaries around how and when you interact with these individuals.

Contract # 2:

• I will be an _____ (attorney, doctor, accountant) just as every other member of my family before has been.

This contract may have been formed from a very early age. You were groomed for the position by spending time in _____'s law firm, on hospital rounds, or at the CPA firm. You were told how wonderful an attorney, doctor or CPA you would make. You were discouraged from some early passions for art, writing, nature or athletics. There was always the underlying assumption you would carry on the tradition. You didn't want to disappoint anyone, so you went off to law or medical school or sat through the licensing exam for your CPA license.

There might have even been subtle hints from your unconscious that, perhaps, this wasn't really what you wanted to be doing. You might have had to take the exam three times before you passed because you just couldn't get into it. You might have passed out at the first sight of blood in the ER. You get physically ill when you think of having to defend a corporation that is raping the environment—an issue you used to have great passion for—but as _____ pointed out, it didn't make the kind of money you were capable of making.

Not becoming who you were expected to become would have meant a lifetime of jokes, family disdain and grief. That's why you went along with it.

You aren't sure whether or not the reasons are still valid, but your health is beginning to suffer by the stress of the long hours and the fact that you are being asked to work out of congruence with who you really are. You know you are no longer being served by the contract.

Again, this awareness is the first step in changing your life. The second is making a conscious decision to discover who you truly are and what it is you really want to do.

Contract #3:

- I cannot pursue my dreams of becoming a _____(veterinarian, police officer, business owner) because those aren't suitable jobs for women in my family.

You many not think that there are any of these types of contracts around anymore. They are left over from earlier years when such statements were common. I would say that far fewer of the contracts get started today, but they still exist.

The same reinforcement pattern followed as well-meaning parents discouraged their daughters from becoming who or what they wanted to be. The were directed to more suitable occupations such as nursing or teaching. If you are a man who held a passionate desire to teach or to go to nursing school, you may have found that you were discouraged from going into such a "female" world.

I am heartened that so many did, in fact, follow their dreams. I know many wonderful, nurturing male nurses and teachers and competent female doctors, police officers and business owners.

Think about your own unwritten contracts . Whom were they with? Take some time to write them down

Contract   With Whom:

_____   _____

_____   _____

_____   _____

_____   _____

_____   _____

_____   _____

_____   _____

_____   _____

Take a good look at them.When were they formed? How have they been reinforced? How have you continued to allow them to be reinforced? What were the reasons behind this? What would you have lost if you had broken the contract? Are these reasons still valid? Are you still being served by hanging on to the contract?

_____

_____

I urge you to begin a dialogue with yourself and seriously answer these questions. Remember, having the awareness that the contract exists is half the battle. Once you have the awareness you can then begin to make conscious choices about if and how you will work with them. I don't believe that we ever truly overcome exotic blocks. We simply make conscious choices about them.

Limiting beliefs are another form of exotic blocks. Some limiting beliefs are so ingrained in society at large, that they take on an almost religious acceptance. One belief in particular is the one that says "artists starve." Well, everyone knows that. Of course they starve. It's part of the official manifestation of becoming an artist. It's a fact. See what I mean?

Don't get me wrong. Some artists want to live simply by choice. Some buy into the belief that poverty and art are fused together, never to part. That's simply not true. You may not make a living by trying to become the next Van Gough (unless you have a brother who is willing to support you and purchase some of your paintings) but you can make a living with your creative expression. They key is not to get stuck on exactly what form it takes.

Other limiting beliefs may be that work has to be hard or that you cannot make a living doing what you love and want to do. I would challenge you to confront these beliefs much like you did the garden variety or factual blocks

Hanging on to your woundedness is another area in which we can sabotage our personal and professional growth. Authors Caroline Myss and Louise Hay have written extensively on this.

Essentially what they are trying to covey, and what I want to underscore, is that when we hang on to our past wounds and when we wear those wounds like badges of honor, we limit our growth—both personally and professionally.

Whether our past includes sexual, physical or psychological abuse, or alcoholism or addiction of any kind, if we too closely identify who we are with what has happened, we are limiting ourselves. We are so much more than our wounds!

This is not to say that these are not serious issues and do not need to be addressed in the safety and security of a therapist's office. They are and they do. AND making them the foundation of our identity robs us of our full potential.

If you have issues that need to be addressed, address them. Then, choose to take back your own power and live your life according to your plans. It may not have been your choice at a younger age. It is your choice now.

Barriers to Your Own Success

When any of these blocks are not identified and challenged, quite often you will discover that you begin to build barriers to your own success. These barriers prevent you from taking the steps necessary to achieve your goals. They may look like:

- You wait for the "perfect" time to start something

- You only try it if you know you can succeed.

- You procrastinate (you don't quite get that bid in on time).

- You decide to take care of others and put their needs before yours. (which is handy, because you can then blame them for what you don't accomplish).

- You stay in your "comfort" zone.

- You expect immediate results.

- You blame others for your situation.

- You stay in a "victim" role instead of making conscious choices to see and do life differently.

- You focus on the negative and on what's not working, instead of what is working.

- You fail to see the opportunity that lies within what's not working.

- You expect to fail.

- You keep doing what you know doesn't work.

- You beat yourself up mentally .

- You ignore your intuition, your inner yearnings and desires.

    I've listed these here so that you can begin to "call" yourself on some of them. Doing this will help you identify the blocks behind them. Can you identify some barriers you've thrown up to sabotage your own success?

_____
_____
_____
_____
_____
_____
_____

Risks: Doing Life Differently

I truly believe that in order for each of us to realize our full potential as human beings—in both our personal and professional lives—we need to be able to take risks.

Risk—in the context that I use the word—refers to stepping outside of your comfort zone to do something differently.

Imagine being a gerbil. Everyday you get up, go outside and get on your gerbil wheel. You are comfortable in knowing that each step will lead to another, identical step and will result in the same known facts that they always do. You know what each moment in your day, your week, your life will look like. It will always look the same. While there can be a sense of comfort and an illusion of control in such a scenario, there is also the reality of stagnation.

When I think of risk, I always envision one of Sandra Boynton's cartoon character greeting cards where a hippo in a tutu is poised at the end of a diving board ready to jump into a tiny pool of water. The caption reads "No guts. No Glory."

If we do not risk doing life differently . . . getting off that gerbil wheel, or diving into life, we do not fully experience all that life has to offer—both in pain and in pleasure. If we did not experience life's pain—be it in the form of rejection, failure or loss, we would not be able to appreciate life's joys.

We, as Americans, are so willing to risk billions of dollars on a daily basis in the stock market. The pay off is financial growth. But when it comes to risking our "selves," we turn and run as fast as we can. We don't see any reward in baring our souls or taking a risk on a personal basis. We only see potential embarrassment...not the enriching growth that can actually take place.

Even in failure, in loss, in baring our souls to another come gifts. They are often difficult gifts, but they are gifts.

Learning to Take Risks

You've played it safe all of your life. Now, you want to begin to really live your life! You want to get off that gerbil wheel and do life differently but you're afraid you will never be able to change! Don't worry—there's hope! You can learn to take risks!

You don't have to take one giant step for human-kind all at once. In fact, I wouldn't even recommend it if you are not a natural risk-taker to begin with. I would break it down into six steps.

Step One:

Identify the block or blocks that are holding you back. Write down the risks you would take in overcoming them.

Step Two:

Make a conscious decision to begin taking calculated risks in either working with or transcending your block or blocks.

Step Three:

List the risks in a series of steps that you will take to begin to work with the blocks. Start with less threatening risks and work up to larger ones. I have suggested to individuals to begin taking risks in areas not associated with their goals, simply to break old habits and get them used to doing things differently. For example:

- Take a different way home from work.

- Switch your checking account to another bank.

- Shop at a different grocery store.

Step Four:

Keep a list of your accomplishments and take time to reflect upon them. When you have a day in which you can't possibly take another risk and are beating yourself up about it, pull out your list of accomplishments and pat yourself on the back and acknowledge just how far you have come.

Step Five:

Enlist the encouraging support of friends, family and co-workers with whom you feel safe. Often times, the simple act of voicing your fears will cause them to lose their power over you and you will be able to take the risk and move beyond the fear.

Step Six:

Practice taking risks in all areas of your life.

• Ask someone out. Don't be attached to the outcome. Your goal is to simply "ask."

• Voice your opinion in a large group.

• Try something new each week for dinner.

• Take a class on something about which you know nothing.

Okay, it's your turn. In your notebook, write in your answers for each step. Use as many lines as you need.

Step one:
Blocks holding me back: The risk in overcoming
                            them:

_____   _____

_____   _____

_____   _____

_____   _____

_____   _____

Step two:
I will make a conscious decision to work on the following blocks:

_____

_____

_____

_____

Step three:
These are risks, not associated with my goals, that I will begin taking to break established patterns or "habits" in my life:

_____

_____

_____

_____

These are the risks associated with my blocks I will take to work with or overcome my blocks:

Step four:
My list of accomplishments:

Step five:
Family, friends and co-workers I'll ask for support:

Step six:

Risks in other areas of my life that I will take:

_____

_____

_____

_____

_____

What I am really asking you to do is to begin to re-frame how you view risks. Risks are opportunities for growth, new experiences and life lessons.

When you can break out of your old comfortable ways of doing and being, you open yourself up to so much more of the richness that life has to offer—on all levels!

Who are You and What do You Want Your Life to Stand For?

It's time to get back to center. It takes a great deal of courage to identify blocks. Beyond that, it includes taking risks in working to overcome or integrate them.

By revisiting the questions "who am I?" and "what do I want my life to stand for?" you are re-connecting to the reasons why you choose to go beyond your blocks and affirm that you are truly more than your old wounds.

Take a moment and write in your notebook the ways in which working to overcome your blocks will help you achieve your goals, live life in congruence with who you are and support what it is you want your life to stand for.

_____

_____

_____

_____

_____

Chapter 6

Demolition Crews and Architects of Change

*Thus to be independent of pubic opinion
is the first formal condition of achieving
anything great...*

G.W.F. Hegel
From *Zen and the Art of Making a Living*
by Laurence G. Bolt

Truly wonderful things can be achieved when we work in a spirit of cooperation with others. However, in order to achieve our individual goals and reach our full potential, we need to stand apart from the collective beliefs and opinions of others. In other words, we can take in the advice and experience of others, but in the end, we are the ones who actually have to live our lives for ourselves. We have our own best answers for how we do this.

I state this first, because there will be others who think they have our own best answers. They've been there, done that, or may have known someone who has. They know what's best for us…what will work and what won't work. And, they have no qualms about telling you your plan won't work. I call these folks members of the demolition crew.

Each of us has our own, private, demolition crew. Isn't that special? Our demolition crews are made up of often well-meaning individuals who are unconsciously trying to undermine our goals and dreams. Demolition crews may also contain individuals who make conscious attempts to sabotage our success.

Demolition Tactics and the Reasons Behind Them

The members of our crew who act in an unconscious manner may include close friends, family members, current or former co-workers, suppliers, enhancers, clients or customers. They could be anyone. On the surface, they seem sincere, are supportive and offer a broad-base of encouragement, *and,* they can also plant subtle seeds of doubt in our minds. Their comments might go something like this:

"I think it's wonderful you're doing this! I'm SOOO excited for you. You know, Joe, down the street tried to do this last year. He lost his shirt, but I know you will be able to make it work!"

"I know you've been doing this in your old position, and I know you'll be great on your own, but if you're just going to do the same thing, wouldn't you feel more comfortable with a secure job and benefits?"

"I know you've been doing this as a hobby for a few years, and do beautiful work, but do you really think you can support yourself doing this full time? You know, though, I'll support any decision you make."

"I think it's wonderful that you're following your bliss. Wouldn't it be great if we could all throw caution to the wind, forget our responsibilities and live life like that!"

Some of these comments may or may not seem familiar. Your comments may be specific to your situation. Whatever the case may be you can recognize them by noting how you feel inside when something is said.

When you start to listen with awareness, you'll begin picking up on the subtleties behind what is actually being said. Many times what is happening is that the well-meaning person is projecting his or her fears on your situation.

Your Mom heard that Joe went belly-up doing what she thought was the same thing you're doing. What she might not have known was: Did Joe do the research, have the passion, talent and values for the job? Did he have the experience or drive necessary to make it work? Did he really want to make it work? You are You. Joe is Joe.

When your best friend asks if you'd be more comfortable with a stable income and set benefits, what he or she is really saying is that they would be more comfortable with a stable income and set benefits…well, at least the perception of a stable income and set benefits. These days, nothing is that sacred.

The co-worker who wonders if you can really support yourself with your hobby may be a bit jealous that you are taking the risk to do so. That person may even become angry at him or her-self for not being able to do something similar and displace that anger toward you.

Your success can threaten others with a less than strong sense of self. Your success, or even perceived success, forces them take a look at themselves. Often, many people don't like what they see. Their disappointment, resentment or even anger can be misdirected toward you in the form of subtle (or not so subtle) comments that can serve as waves against your cliffs of confidence.

Another example is the individual who thinks it's great that you are following your bliss but shirking your responsibilities. There's a lot of anger behind that statement. Perhaps that person would love to follow his or her bliss, but has made choices early on in life that resulted in a bit more responsibility that you may have. Or, you've found a way to manage doing what you want to do AND remain responsible to your personal and financial commitments.

While we may be able to recognize when these statements are being made and, we may even truly know what's behind them or where they are coming from, they can often still affect us.

Let's say on one particular day you've received 200 positive comments about yourself, your business, your way of doing things. Wow! That's especially validating because you began that day questioning your competence and expertise. Let's also say that somewhere along the line, you received one negative comment from a member of your demolition crew. Despite the fact that you've gotten validation from 200 people, it's the one negative comment that you hold onto and focus on. That's all it takes to water those few toxic seeds of self-doubt!

You soon begin to integrate these comments. Those old "tapes" start running and steadily erode our self esteem. "Who do I think I am to think I can actually do this?" "Maybe she was right, I really won't make much of myself." "I should have stayed in that job with good benefits and decent salary. I wasn't happy, but work isn't supposed to be fun, right?"

They key is to know and understand what's behind comments from the unconscious members of your crew. Tell yourself "it's their stuff." You may have to do this a number of times before you truly begin to believe it. However, the more you practice it and the more you begin to know and understand where a particular person is coming from, the better equipped you'll be to withstand the comments they make.

Identifying Members of Your Personal Demolition Crew

Identifying members of your personal entourage can be tricky because many of them are, for the most part, very supportive people. They've been with you through the struggle of making the decision to start your own business, they've fed you when you didn't have the money to pay your own way, they've encouraged you with inspiring words and they have given their undeniable commitment to be with you through thick and thin. AND, they have their own stuff about what you're doing.

You can start to identify members of your private crew by listening to what is said and thinking about what is behind it. Why would they have made the comment they made that caused you to reconsider what you were doing?

Talk to them about their (perhaps lost) dreams and ambitions. Ask them what's missing for them in their work and personal lives. Find out what's going on in their lives. They may have had aspirations that, because of life choices or circumstances, were never realized. They may have fears of loss of financial security, or limiting beliefs (like artists starve or work has to be hard) that are secretly making their way into seemingly supportive statements.

Some of these individuals are very good friends and close family members of yours. It's hard to think that they would actually be trying to undermine what you've worked so hard to do.

The short explanation is—they're not consciously trying to do it. Again, knowing, understanding and working with this will help you maintain long-standing friendships. However, you may need to set some boundaries around these relationships.

Now, as I mentioned before there may be people who will consciously try to sabotage your success. These people, too, may try to present themselves as "friends" or supportive former co-workers. However, he or she may also have ideas of success for him or herself and YOU becoming successful is a perceived threat to their success. I don't think these people are common, but they do exist. Many of them are so insecure that they have to think of ways to undermine you so that they can shine. Once you've identified these individuals, I would say it's best to try to avoid them when possible.

Setting Boundaries Around Toxic Relationships or Letting Go of Them

Once you've been able to identify members of your demolition crew, it would be wise to establish how, or if, you want to relate to them in the future.

Members of your crew who also happen to be family members can be the most difficult around which to set boundaries. They are, after all, family. Setting boundaries around friends you see often and who ask about you and your business can also be challenging.

There are some fairly easy ways in which to set boundaries around those with whom you want to continue relationships.

First, you can try to limit the scope of your conversation as it relates to your business. Try to keep the conversation personal or focused on them. If a "how's the business going?" question arises, you can respond with generic statements like "it's building.," "The big picture looks good.," or, "I'm making some great contacts." Statements like these allow you to answer the question, but avoid specific information. Don't give them information that they can use in negative statements. You don't need that!

Again, I want to reiterate that these people truly mean well. Many don't understand how their "stuff" can be projected onto your situation. AND, you don't need that!

Another way in which to set boundaries is to limit the kinds of activities you engage in with these individuals. Going to films or concerts leaves little time for "business" conversation. Don't ask these people to help you with business projects. You don't have to leave them out of the loop, but you can control how and when you interact with them.

Some relationships, however, may need to be severed. Have you ever been in a relationship where you've found yourself walking on egg shells simply trying to keep the other person happy? If you said or did the right thing (which could vary from day to day), you were in the good graces of this person. If, by chance, you said the wrong thing—although last week, it might have been the right thing—you automatically became the object of this person's anger and rage. You may have backed off for a bit and even extended an olive leaf in hopes of mending whatever it was that you did wrong—you're never really quite sure—but apparently, you have done something wrong. Your friend may have even recognized his or her outburst as a bit of an over-reaction and has showered gifts upon you. Everything seems back in balance…until the next time you say or do something wrong and the whole thing starts all over again. Do you have anyone like this in your life?

Despite your best attempts, you keep getting yourself into the same situations with these people. These people may or may not be "typical" members of your demolition crew, but they are members. They take away (and you give them) a tremendous amount of energy that could be directed toward your success.

Have faith. There is actually a theory based on these types of relationships. It's called the drama triangle. First developed in the late 1960's by Stephen Karpman, the drama triangle was expanded upon by Marsha Utain, M.S. and Dr. Arthur Melville. (I've noted their booklet in the bibliography).

The basic triangle involves two people, with one person playing either the "good guy" or "bad guy" role. The other person is the "victim" or, the one calling the shots.

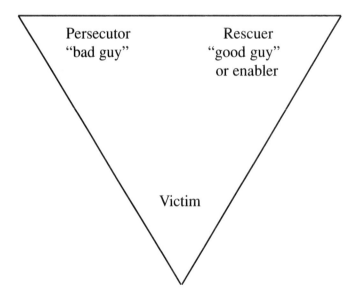

The "victim" takes no responsibility for his actions or feelings and will place the blame on everyone else (i.e., the world, "them," you) if things aren't going well in his life. They tend to use guilt to get you to do what it is they want you to do. When you do, you are their best friend and are well-paid in the form of kindness, gifts and praise. When you try to step out of the triangle and live your life for yourself, you become the "bad guy" and can be subject to some pretty difficult bouts of anger and persecution. It's this anger and persecution that keeps you actively engaged in the triangle because you keep trying to make the person feel better.

It truly is a draining situation to be in. However, once you are able to realize what's going on, you can make a decision about how or if you are going to continue a relationship with these individuals. I have had two such friendships in the past. I made the decision to end both. I decided the time and energy that was required to sustain them wasn't worth it and that continuing to maintain them was taking away positive energy I wanted to be using to build a business and reach some personal goals. It was a difficult decision to make and I still feel the loss of the authentic part of the friendship.

If you have people in your life that fit into this category, you must make the decision for yourself.

How to have Trust in Yourself (When No One Else Around You Seems To)

In Deepak Chopra's book, *The Seven Spiritual Laws of Success,* he speaks of living life from a point of self-referral. He says that when we do this we are closer to our own true nature and, therefore, closer to achieving our full potential.

It's a difficult proposition to live life that way. Think of all the outside influences that we encounter every day. There are situations and circumstances that require we respond in "appropriate" ways (meaning by someone else's standards). And, there are people from whom we would like to gain approval. Again, we might change our natural or authentic response.

When we change our responses and actions to impress others, we are operating from our ego. There are times in life when we make conscious choices to operate from that base. However, when we're ambivalent about something, or need to tap into what it is we really think and feel about a certain situation, we need to be able to call upon and rely on our own point of self-referral.

When we are operating from this base the power of our convictions becomes more apparent. Our true or authentic self radiates confidence, sense of self, passion and compassion. People are naturally drawn to us because they sense our integrity and trustworthiness.

We are conditioned to listen and respond to the comments of others. We want to fit in. We want to be loved, admired, respected and looked up to. In order to do this, we quite often believe that we have to squeeze ourselves into a pre-determined mold. We begin to form our bodies and our souls in the shape that is required to secure these things. We become reactive to the praises, comments and criticisms of others. Our thoughts, actions, beliefs and goals are all based upon pleasing others. We may end up getting what we think we want but at what cost? We get these things at the expense of our authentic selves. Somewhere along the line, we lost track of that person. We may not even remember who that person was or the things that brought passion and joy into our lives.

It truly takes courage to be who you are…to, as Henry David Thoreau said—march to the beat of your own drum. It is much easier and safer to follow the crowd and the pre-determined path to their definition of success.

How do you maintain balance in listening to the needs of your own voice? People do it in various ways. Many meditate, some engage in a solitary physical activity, others might have a connecting poem, daily affirmation, or piece of music that can remind them that they have a voice in the midst of all the chaos. Fox's Alley McBeal has a theme song that reminds her of her own strength.

Starting a Professional Group of Creative, Supportive Entrepreneurs

Another way in which to support yourself and help others in maintaining their own inner voice and direction is to start a professional group of creative entrepreneurs. I don't mean a support group in the traditional sense of the word, but I am talking about a group of people whose purpose is to support and empower each other in the unique way.

I would have between four and six members to the group with diverse business interests. I would also try to get a mix of individuals whose talents lie in different areas of business so that you are able to draw upon the strengths of each member. That way, if one member of the group needs to address a marketing, accounting or employee issue, there is at least one member of the group whose expertise lies in that area.

Mentors and Other Sources of Support and Inspiration.

A mentor is someone who supports and leads you—always by example and sometimes quite literally—through the maze of trials and celebrations that encompass your success.

A mentor is an individual who offers words of wisdom and inspiration and encourages us to remain true to our selves as we struggle to make decisions that will affect our life and career.

A mentor is quite often someone for whom you hold a great deal of admiration and respect.

Some people have established formal mentoring relationships with individuals who see their potential and passion. Some of these relationships are less formal, but are supportive, encouraging relationships none the less.

How would you go about trying to establish a formal or informal mentoring relationship? The first thing I would ask you to do is to make a list of individuals you know whom you admire. To the right of the list, write down the characteristics or qualities you admire in that person.

Name   Characteristics or Qualities I Admire:

_____   _____

_____   _____

_____   _____

_____   _____

_____   _____

_____   _____

_____   _____

_____   _____

_____   _____

After you've done this, ask yourself what characteristics and qualities would I like to have in a mentor? A good mentor will be true to him or herself and encourage you to make decisions based on who you are. Your mentor will have integrity, be trustworthy and respectful. A good mentor will also be able to help you see and understand how what it is you do in life can enhance the lives of others and encourage this.

Are there any individuals you'd like to approach to establish a formal or informal mentoring relationship? Some will be involved with other relationships and may not have the time right now but I believe that all of them will be flattered that you've asked.

Sometimes these relationships happen naturally. I was taking a class in broadcast journalism when one of my instructors said "Hey, kid. You can write." He took it upon himself to take me under his wing and guide me in becoming a better writer and give me insights into the field of radio journalism. (Thanks, Phil).

Not all of us are bestowed with the good fortune of having a living, breathing mentor. However, all of us have access to what author Marsha Sinetar calls the "Mentor's Spirit." The mentor's spirit is any life affirming influence in someone's life.

Sinetar describes the mentor's spirit as anything that affirms "a way of being or thinking that inspires us to be authentically ourselves." It's unique to the individual. This kind of inspiration might be found in music, art, nature, classic literature, sacred scriptures, film, physical movement or a combination. I have a friend who—when he feels a need to connect with that life affirming energy—goes skiing.

Again, connecting to life-affirming energy is different for everyone. I tend to reconnect through literature, sacred scriptures, inspirational lectures and through sharing thoughts and dreams with dear friends.

What people, places or things bring life affirming energy to you? Make it a point to reconnect with them on a regular basis. These "events" or actions will help you find calm amidst chaos and quite often will provide the inspiration and insight needed to take your next step.

I'd now like you to go back for a moment and revisit the list of names of those whom you admire. Sometimes it surprises people to learn that they possess that same list of characteristics and qualities which they admire in others. It's true! We aren't able to recognize a quality in someone else without possessing it ourselves. It may lie as only a seed of desire that needs to be watered, but it's there.

Who Are You and What Do You Want Your Life to Stand For?

Here we are again for the last time. By revisiting the questions "who am I?" and "what do I want my life to stand for?" you are now underscoring your ability to trust your own voice and intuition. You are affirming your commitment to finding mentors or other life affirming people, places or things that will honor and support who you are and respect what it is you want your life to stand for and how it is you want to live your life.

Please take your notebook and prepare a final version of the answers to these questions. Consider the answers in each chapter and combine them for a complete picture.

You may wish to write them on a computer, print them out and post them in a location that you will see every day. These are powerful words. They are your words. They are a validation that we truly do have our own answers—we simply need only ask the right questions.

Conclusion

As I re-read these words, I find I still want to change, add or edit things. The challenge with putting words to paper is that I know they may be perceived as static. We, as human beings, are dynamic. We are always changing. As we gain new knowledge and life experience our ideas and beliefs expand accordingly.

I also know that this book is a reflection—a snap-shot if you will—of the ideals, beliefs and passions I hold at this moment.

Central in those ideals and passions is the belief that personal fulfillment and professional success is an inside job. Fulfillment, meaning, purpose and success are built from a foundation of self-knowledge. Self-knowledge is power and it is empowering. It also reminds us that we do have our own answers...we simply need to ask the questions.

My hope is that you have gained new knowledge about yourself and have been inspired to live you life on a more authentic level. I also hold hope that you have discovered ways in which to bring elements of yourself to your work...allowing work—your business—to be natural expression of who you are.

I've purposely re-stated the questions "who are you?" and "what do you want your life to stand for?" at the end of each chapter to serve as a reminder that you do not have to get caught up on a corporate gerbil wheel. What often happens when we decide to go it on our own is that we step off of one gerbil wheel right onto another...this one of our own making.

I've asked these questions as a way of going back to center—a way to stay connected with your personal values and goals and your unique definition of success. The questions are also meant to serve as a gentle reminder of the things that bring you joy and happiness and how you want to live your life.

I want to leave you with words, not of my own, but words which resonate with my soul, and inspire me to surround myself with supportive, caring visionaries and friends:

Stay often in the company of dreamers.
They believe you can achieve things which
are impossible.
                              Mary Anne Radmacher-Hershey.

Bibliography

Baker, Joel (1992). *Paradigms.* New York: HarperBusiness.

Bradenburger, A. and Nalebuff, B.J. (1996). *Co-opetition.* New York: Bantam Doubleday Dell Publishing.

Briskin, Alan (1996). *The Stirring of the Soul in the Workplace.* San Francisco: Jossey-Bass.

Burns, David (1980). *Feeling Good: The New Mood Therapy.* New York: Avon

Carlson, Richard (1997). *Don't Sweat the Small Stuff.* New York: Hyperion.

Carlson, Richard and Bailey, Joseph (1997). *Slowing Down to the Speed of Life.* San Francisco: HarperCollins.

Chopra, Deepak (1993).*The Seven Spiritual Laws of Success.* San Rafael, CA: Amber-Allen Publishing.

Covey, Stephen R. (1989). *The 7 Habits of Highly Effective People.* NY: Fireside/Simon and Schuster.

Csikszentimihaly, Mihaly (1990). *Flow: The Psychology of Optimal Experience.* NY: HarperCollins.

Das, Lama Sura (1997). *Awakening the Buddha Within.* NY: Bantam Doubleday Dell.

Dreher, Diane. (1996). *The Tao of Personal Leadership.* New York: HarperBusiness.

Edwards, Paul and Sarah. (1997). *Teaming Up.* NY: Tarcher Putnam.

—— (1991). *Getting Business to Come to You.* NY: Tarcher Perigee.

—— (1990). *Working from Home.* NY: Tarcher Perigee.

Falkenstein, Lynda (1996). *Nichecraft: Using your Specialness to Focus your Business, Corner your Market, and Make Customers Seek You Out.* New York: HarperBusiness.

Gorin, Fern (1995). *The Life Purpose Process.* San Diego: Life Purpose Institute.

Hillman, James. (1996). *The Soul's Code.* New York: Random House.

Jeffers, Susan (1987). *Feel the Fear and Do It Anyway.* New York: Ballantine Books.

Jones, Laurie Beth. (1996). *The Path: Creating your Mission Statement for Life and Work.* NY: Hyperion.

Jung, Carl G. (1933). *Modern Man in Search of a Soul.* NY: Harcourt Brace Javanovich.

Levinson, Jay Conrad. (1995). *Guerrilla Marketing for the Home-Based Business.* NY: Houghton Mifflin Company

—— (1993). *Guerrilla Marketing Excellence.* NY: Houghton Mifflin Co.

Myss, Caroline 1997). *Why People Don't Heal.* New York: Harmony Books

Orman, Suze. (1997). *The 9 Steps to Financial Freedom.* New York: Crown Publishers

Popcorn, Faith (1996). *Clicking.* New York: HarperCollins

Sinetar, Marsha (1987) *Do what you Love, the Money will Follow.* NY: Dell Books

—— (1986). *Ordinary People as Monks and Mystics.* Mahwah, NJ: Paulist Press.

——(1998). *The Mentor's Spirit*. Boulder, CO: Sounds True.

Toms, J.W. and Toms, Michael (1998) *True Work: The Sacred Dimension of Earning A Living*. NY: Bell Tower

Utain, Marsha (undated) (booklet). *Stepping out of Chaos*. Deerfield Beach, FL: Health Communication.

The words Mary Anne Radmacher-Hershey have been used with permission. Ms. Radmacher-Hershey's words, art and unique creations are available at:

words, ink
12th and N.E. Broadway
Portland, OR 97232
503-284-4212

words, ink
255 N. Hemlock
Cannon Beach, OR 97110
503-436-2098

radmacher-hershey Gallery
Sandpiper Square—Upstairs
Cannon Beach, OR 97110
502-436-2774

Index

About the Author

Penny Carter is a small business marketing and career consultant operating under the name of Creating A Life.

Penny's passion is to empower and inspire others to define themselves according their own unique nature and to understand how self-knowledge holds the key to personal fulfillment and professional success.

Penny holds a degree in social science (psychology) from Marylhurst College and is a member of the National Career Development Counselors. Penny is a certified Life Purpose Process©* career consultant.

Her career background includes journalism, marketing, public relations, event production and speaking on children's grief issues.

In addition to writing and managing her marketing business, Penny facilitates groups and works with businesses in Building A Business—Creating A Life, Finding your Life's True Work, Living and Working Authentically, Employee Enrichment Programs, and Getting more Bang for your College Buck.

She is also a guest lecturer and inspirational speaker.

Penny resides in Portland, Oregon.

For information on training or workshops, please call Creating A Life (503) 249-8372, send an email to: creatingalife@teleport.com , or write Creating A Life, P.O. Box 18179, Portland, OR 97218.

*The Life Purpose Process© was developed by Fern Gorin, M.A. and the Life Purpose Institute in San Diego, California. This process has been successfully utilized with over 12,000 people.

To order additional copies of

Building a Business
Creating a Life

Book: $12.95   Shipping/Handling: $3.50

Contact: **SPIRIT PRESS**
3324 N.E. Peerless Place
Portland, Oregon 97232
Fax: 503-235-8135
Phone: 800-507-2665
E-mail: spiritp@teleport.com